Advanced Introduction to Public Management and Administration

Elgar Advanced Introductions are stimulating and thoughtful introductions to major fields in the social sciences and law, expertly written by the world's leading scholars. Designed to be accessible yet rigorous, they offer concise and lucid surveys of the substantive and policy issues associated with discrete subject areas.

The aims of the series are two-fold: to pinpoint essential principles of a particular field, and to offer insights that stimulate critical thinking. By distilling the vast and often technical corpus of information on the subject into a concise and meaningful form, the books serve as accessible introductions for undergraduate and graduate students coming to the subject for the first time. Importantly, they also develop well-informed, nuanced critiques of the field that will challenge and extend the understanding of advanced students, scholars and policy-makers.

Titles in the series include:

International Political Economy
Benjamin J. Cohen

The Austrian School of Economics
Randall G. Holcombe

Cultural Economics
Ruth Towse

Law and Development
Michael J. Trebilcock and Mariana Mota Prado

International Humanitarian Law
Robert Kolb

International Tax Law
Reuven S. Avi-Yonah

Post Keynesian Economics
J.E. King

International Intellectual Property
Susy Frankel and Daniel J. Gervais

Public Management and Administration
Christopher Pollitt

International Conflict and Security Law
Nigel D. White

Comparative Constitutional Law
Mark Tushnet

International Human Rights Law
Dinah L. Shelton

Entrepreneurship
Robert D. Hisrich

International Trade Law
Michael J. Trebilcock

Public Policy
B. Guy Peters

The Law of International Organizations
Jan Klabbers

International Environmental Law
Ellen Hey

International Sales Law
Clayton P. Gillette

Advanced Introduction to

Public Management and Administration

CHRISTOPHER POLLITT

Emeritus Professor, Public Governance Institute, Katholieke Universiteit Leuven, Belgium

Elgar Advanced Introductions

PUBLISHING

Cheltenham, UK • Northampton, MA, USA

Published by
Edward Elgar Publishing Limited
The Lypiatts
15 Lansdown Road
Cheltenham
Glos GL50 2JA
UK

Edward Elgar Publishing, Inc.
William Pratt House
9 Dewey Court
Northampton
Massachusetts 01060
USA

A catalogue record for this book
is available from the British Library

Library of Congress Control Number: 2015954322

Printed on elemental chlorine free (ECF)
recycled paper containing 30% Post-Consumer Waste

ISBN 978 1 78471 231 0 (cased)
ISBN 978 1 78471 233 4 (paperback)
ISBN 978 1 78471 232 7 (eBook)

Typeset by Servis Filmsetting Ltd, Stockport, Cheshire
Printed and bound in the USA

For Hilkka, one more time.

Contents

Tables

Preface

If you want to deal directly with matters of pressing international, national and local concern, then study public management. If you would like to do field research that involves meeting dedicated, highly skilled professionals working for a fairer, less hazardous and more caring society, then study public management. If you are interested in where all the taxpayers' money goes, and how people are held accountable for its spending (or not), then study public management. If you are interested in the causes and effects of government corruption, and wonder why some countries are evidently far more prone to this cancer than others, then study public management. If you want to know more about the largest and most powerful organizations that have existed for the last hundred years, then study public management.

On the other hand, if you want to work on a topic that some people will regard as ineffably boring and anorak-ish, then study public management. If you want to have difficulty at cocktail parties explaining in a few words exactly what your subject is, then study public management. Of course, it is always possible that if you study public management you may not be invited to many cocktail parties.

This book is about a Janus-faced subject, which famously suffers from a recurrent identity crisis. In fact it is more than Janus-faced, because Janus only had two, opposing faces, whereas public management sometimes seems to have many. It is a fascinating and infuriating subject, sometimes both at once.

"Why infuriating?", I hear someone ask. For a variety of reasons. One is the tendency towards narrow scholasticism which has been visible recently in some parts of our academic community. But far more infuriating than this is the incessant privileging, by the mass media, of issues of political personalities and broad political doctrines, over issues of practical organization. Accurate reporting on more mundane administrative questions, it seems to me, would frequently matter more in the daily lives of most citizens than what politician A said about politician B yesterday, or whether someone is "for" or "against" the European Union. Instead, why not ask whether this programme or project has worked, for whom, how and why? To put it crudely: it is easy to sound off with opinions about how the world should be and considerably more difficult to organize that desired world into existence. Yet the mass media pay far, far more attention to the former than the latter, and usually only focus on the organizing bit when something has gone badly wrong. We – the public – are therefore treated to an endless diet of ephemeral politics and organizational failure, while the crucial "how to" details are seldom discussed at all (and success stories are often ignored, especially if they are the type that involves reliable, gradually improving service over time). This media bias is one important reason why the subject of public management is sometimes regarded as boring.

The sheer size and importance of public management/public administration is hard to overestimate. During the 1980s there was much talk of "rolling back the state" and, in particular, the need to reduce the size of the welfare state – this discourse echoed across North America and many (but not all) European countries. Then, since the banking crisis of 2008, and the consequent economic and fiscal crises, Europe and North America once again heard many calls to shrink the public sector. Yet despite many changes and challenges, and much real pain, the public sector remains both large and important throughout the developed world. In the 2015 edition of one of the most authoritative international comparisons, the Organisation for Economic Co-operation and Development's (OECD) *Government at a Glance,* we find that public spending on average accounts for more than 41 per cent of the gross domestic product (GDP), with France and most of the Nordic countries well over 50 per cent, and few countries below 30 per cent. On average, the public sector directly employs more than 21 per cent of the total labour force (and many more as contracted-out employees). In the Nordic group the figure is at or near 30 per cent. Interestingly, citizens in most OECD member states tend to have quite high trust in public services such as education, healthcare and the police, but considerably lower trust in national governments, together with minimal trust in political parties and journalists. (Yet it is the politicians and the journalists that we hear most from.) And if we look to the future, who can envisage any solution to the challenges of, say, climate change or mass migration or future disease pandemics without governments and inter-governmental bodies playing crucial roles? Given these broad facts, the study of public management seems central.

Because the field is multi-faceted, multi-disciplinary and multi-theoretical, there would be many ways of writing an Advanced Introduction such as this. There is no God-like position from which to look down on all the different approaches and factions, and pronounce a final judgement on each. To write this book entirely from within one such partial perspective would be a disservice to readers, who deserve more than one "angle" on such a complex territory. Thus I faced an authorial dilemma. I could not unify the field with One Best Perspective but neither would it be right to retreat into the neck of the woods I myself happen most frequently to inhabit, and simply describe and promote that corner alone. While there may be no ultimate solution to this dilemma, what I have striven to do is to acknowledge the strengths and weaknesses of a variety of perspectives, and to signal whenever I am "promoting" my own preferred way of looking at things. To signal in this way seemed better than to pretend that I was standing on the peak of that (unavailable) Olympus – at least it warns readers that there are other arguments, ideas and methods available within the public management community. My references include many of these. Yet it remains true that I advance a particular perspective. My defence for this is twofold. First, so does almost every other public management writer, whether they acknowledge it or not. Second, by acknowledging it, I make the text both more transparent and, I would argue, more interesting to read.

The book has also been shaped by my conviction that the "out there" world of the public sector matters (or should matter) a great deal to the public management academic community. We academics need to strive to maintain a continuing balance between our own, proper academic concerns and engagement with what is going on in intergovernmental bodies, governments, public agencies and the vast constellation of organizations involved in the delivery and regulation of public services. This may at first seem a strange thing to be saying – how could public management academics *not* be focused on the real world? Yet often they are not. Some of the internal incentives within the academic world can direct attention elsewhere – to particular kinds of publication, to currently fashionable theories that have little purchase in the real world or to an obsession with methodological purity rather than producing interesting and relevant research findings. These tensions will be acknowledged and explored in what follows, and space will be given to external, "real world" developments as well as to contemporary academic concerns.

So what readers are getting here is – inevitably – somewhat coloured by my own ideas and experiences, which I can only plead are not stultifyingly narrow. I have worked as a civil servant myself, in roles having frequent contacts with ministers, and as an academic at universities in four different countries, as well as often doing advice work for international organizations and a number of national governments. All these experiences have been highly educational, and each has, in one way or another, influenced my thinking. I hope both the fascination and the frustration engendered by this background communicate themselves on the printed page.

Christopher Pollitt
Jarventaka, Finland, 2015

Acknowledgements

With a book of this broad scope a paragraph or two of acknowledgements can never do full justice to all those who have (wittingly or often unwittingly) helped me to write what follows. I begin, therefore, with an apology to those of you who I have left out. Nothing personal – put it down to advancing years.

Let me next acknowledge those whose work has repeatedly influenced my thinking, and whose mark must therefore somehow lie on or between many lines of this text. I have followed their publications over time, rather as one awaits the next novel from a favourite author. These powerful scholars include Pat Dunleavy, Christopher Hood, Larry Lynn, James March and Johan Olsen.

Second, there is a group who have offered particular insights which I have eagerly taken up and which find their echoes somewhere in the present text. Mark Bovens, Nils Brunsson, John Clarke, Nick Manning, Janet Newman, Ray Pawson, Guy B. Peters, Hal Rainey, Rod Rhodes, Kathleen Thelen, Nick Tilley, Steven van de Walle and James Q. Wilson all fall in this category.

Third, I should mention those with whom I have enjoyed collaborating. In the course of such joint labours, I have learned much of advantage and relevance to an Advanced Introduction. Here I warmly acknowledge Johnston Birchall, Geert Bouckaert, John Clarke, Steve Harrison, Walter Kickert and Sandra van Thiel.

Some colleagues have been generous enough to look at parts of the text in draft. For their unrewarded labours and perceptive comments I salute Gavin Drewry, Don Kettl, Richard Stillman, Colin Talbot and Sandra van Thiel.

Inge Vermeulen (once more) lent her impeccable secretarial skills to the last stage of manuscript preparation.

It is has been an additional pleasure to know (almost) all of the above individuals personally, and to develop friendships with many of them. Professional friendships are a special and deeply rewarding sub-species.

Finally, a major influence, intellectually and in every other way, has been Hilkka Summa-Pollitt. I test all sorts of ideas on her, and she is simultaneously ruthless and merciful. One quality of her mercy is that she never reads anything I have published (partly, I think, because she assumes that she already knows what I will have said).

It should be obvious, but I will say it anyway, that none of the above can be held responsible for anything in this book (and in many cases they may well actively disagree with some of my arguments). All seven chapters are mine and mine alone.

1 What kind of a subject is public management/public administration?

> For forms of government let fools contest;
> Whatever is best administered is best. (Alexander Pope, 1734,
> *Essay on Man: Epistle III: Of the Nature and State of Man,*
> *with Respect to Society*)

> The fact of the matter is that most of the problems that we now face . . .
> are administrative problems. (US President John F. Kennedy at a press
> conference, May 1962, see Lasch, 1978, p. 77)

1.1 The aims of this book

This is an Advanced Introduction to the inter-disciplinary field of public management and administration (hereafter PM and PA). As an introduction it tries to go wide – to cover many aspects of the subject. Thus it is more than a theory book, more than a methods book, more than a history of the development of the subject and more than a description of the current organization and preoccupations of the PM/PA scholarly community. It touches on all these aspects, and attempts to relate them, one to another. It also examines the relationship between the academic world and the world of practice. The intention is that this breadth and connectivity should enable anyone using the book to form an overall picture of academic PM/PA as a working community and a body of ideas and practices. The price, obviously, is that there is not enough room to go into many matters in great depth (or into some matters at all). I try to compensate by including many references to other works where more detailed treatments may be pursued. This observation is particularly relevant to the chapters dealing with theory (Chapter 2) and methods (Chapter 3). In both it is simply impossible to give the reader a good working knowledge of the full range of options. So there is no claim to be comprehensive – that would be very difficult even in a work twice the length of this one. It is, however, feasible to offer a sample of what is going on, and to identify some of the advantages and limitations of commonly used approaches.

As an Advanced Introduction the book is written on the assumption that readers will already know something about the subject. It is aimed at masters and doctoral students, and at academic staff, rather than first degree students. Many of these students will be studying PM or PA per se, but, in addition, it should be suitable for those who are taking management modules in professional degrees such as education, healthcare, social care or police studies. The book is written in a way that I hope will also be helpful to many academic staff, perhaps particularly those in the early or middle stages of their career, whose personal networks may not yet be extensive, and whose subject knowledge may perhaps still be confined mainly to the work they did at masters and especially doctoral levels.

Then there is the world of practice. In my experience most PM/PA practitioners these days do not have the time (or sometimes the temperament) to read books, but perhaps some will have the curiosity to pick this one up, to find out what those academics are up to. Furthermore many PM/PA students at masters and doctoral levels are or have been practitioners themselves, so there is an important overlap between the categories of "student" and "practitioner". For them I would certainly hope that there would be plenty of useful material in the following pages.

In an ideal world the book would be read from beginning to end. In the real world there is no strong reason why readers should not pick out a particular chapter that interests them and just focus on that. I do make some references across chapters, and if you should come across one of these I urge you to follow it up.

In the Preface I warned that I was going to write the book in my own preferred style – informal and argumentative. I have not striven for an Olympian, detached tone because, especially in such a diverse field as PM/PA, I would regard that as a misrepresentation of the character of the academic community and the current state of knowledge. I have, however, attempted to display a wide range of views (in theory, method and so on) so even if readers find some of my own preferences in the text, they will also be alerted to the existence of other views.

There is a point about geographic coverage. PM/PA is studied in many countries. The book tries to reflect this and, indeed, Chapter 4 offers some comments about how the geography of the academic PM/PA community may well be shifting, internationally. American, Australian, Belgian, Brazilian, Canadian, Chinese, Danish, Dutch, Estonian, Finnish, French, German, Hungarian, Italian, Norwegian and Swedish sources are cited. So are a number of publications by international bodies such as the OECD or the World Bank. Yet at the same time it would be false to claim that my text gave somehow equal (or even adequate) treatment to all the various national and linguistic PM/PA communities. Written in English, by an Englishman, it carries an almost inevitable bias towards Anglophone sources, authorities and examples. So it is thoroughly international in intent, but only imperfectly so in practice.

In sum, the book is aimed at a large and varied audience, though one united by their interest in public sector organizations, networks and management. Its core purpose is to describe the ideas, methods, people and institutions which comprise contemporary academic public management and administration. In doing so it registers and comments upon some of the forces and fashions which currently seem to drive the PM/PA community along.

1.2   The nature of the beast

PM/PA is a mongrel subject. There are regular claims that it is suffering from an identity crisis (Raadschelders, 2011, pp. 19–35; Zalmanovitch, 2014), although that does not seem to prevent the vast majority of PM/PA scholars getting on with their jobs. It exists at the intersection of a number of different disciplinary streams. It is an interdisciplinary field unified mainly by its real-world "object of study" – government (or, more broadly and recently, governance). This material focus has given rise to a shared agenda of issues, recognized as significant by most (but not all) scholars in the community.

A further complication is that the subject appears to have two different names – public management (PM) and public administration (PA). I will deal directly with this confusion in the next section.

Academic PM (or public administration/PA) while disciplined, is not itself a discipline. This is not a terribly underprivileged condition because neither are most other social sciences. In terms of theories and methodologies PM/PA has always been pluralist, and remains resolutely so. Again, this is not so different from other social sciences:

> Where public administration is a field of study defined by its material object, its theoretical make-up is a mosaic with a rich variety of theories and conceptualizations about government that are successfully used in public administration scholarship. (Raadschelders, 2011, p. 147)

The theories come from those disciplines which have intermingled to create the contemporary field of PM/PA. These include law, political science, economics, generic management and business studies, organization theory and social psychology. New contributory disciplines may enter (as organization theory did after the Second World War) and others may fall out to travel their separate roads (as, regrettably, law has done in many universities). However, its pluralist character and continuing object of study do not change – or not very much or very fast. A historical perspective and/or an analysis of the contemporary organization of academe make it seem very unlikely that any single discipline or theory will ever become widely acknowledged as dominant. Pluralism (the upside) and fragmentation (the downside) will persist, indeed, they may be increasing (Ferlie et al., 2005). The key difference, perhaps, is that in pluralism the different groupings talk to each other, while in fragmentation they do not.

PM/PA is not by any means a narrow field, exclusively concerned with questions of governmental machinery. "After all, government serves society and the study cannot afford to be disconnected from the major questions about and challenges in the society in which it is embedded" (Raadschelders, 2011, pp. 146–7). "It is not in the organization of public administration in the narrow sense, but in shaping society in the broad sense, rooted in the behavior of citizens and consumers, where the key lies to effective policy . . ." (Bouckaert and Van de Donk, 2010, pp. 13–14). So it most certainly includes the nuts and bolts of public service delivery, but also wider questions of policymaking and "speaking truth to power".

PM/PA is a field with a distinctive relationship to practice and practitioners. This relationship has always been – and remains – very close. In a survey of European PM/PA academics 69 per cent of those who responded to the open question "What impact do you want your work to have?" explicitly cited hoped-for effects in the real world of public administration (Bouckaert and Van de Donk, 2010 – n = 91). Only

31 per cent answered purely in terms of academic objectives. This link is equally, if not more prominent in the USA: "[A] field such as public administration – an applied field – cannot survive without finding ways to bring the insights of both cultures together" (Radin, 2013, p. 1).

Of course this does not mean that academics cannot pursue "pure" academic research, without much, if any, thought for its practical application. Some can and some do (and it essential that this high freedom is preserved, in at least a few places). But these "purists" are a minority, and if they were somehow to dominate the field an important element in its *raison d'être* would be lost. The head of one of the academically most respected European PM/PA research units put it like this:

> PA research needs to remain connected to PA practice. Most of our students will not become academics after graduation, but the public administrators and public sector cadres of the future ... Besides, how in the long run can we legitimize the substantial public spending that goes into academic PA research if we are not able to demonstrate that our field maintains an active and productive dialogue with the world of practice? (Bovens, 2010, p. 125)

Thus the PM/PA stage is quite wide, yet it has its limits. PM/PA is not political science, although it would be an unwise scholar who chose to ignore the political contexts within which management issues arose. PM/PA is not law, even in the "law-heavy" states like Germany or France (although, once more, it would be foolish not to pay attention to those aspects of local, national or international law which bear upon the management issue at hand). PM/PA is not generic management, nor non-profit management, nor brand management, nor leadership studies (see Section 1.4 below). All these are legitimate areas of study, but of themselves they do not yet become PM/PA. The "object of study" in PM/PA needs to be directly related to government or, to use the term which is more widely accepted in continental Europe than in the UK or North America, the state (for an analysis of this long-lasting difference in traditions of thought on opposite sides of the Atlantic, see Rutgers, 2001). "Directly related to" does not mean that it has to confine itself to departments and agencies of government alone. It also covers companies performing work for governments on contract, organizations which partner public agencies, citizens who use public services and so on. Again, generic management, leadership studies and so on *may* uncover interesting findings, but they are only relevant to PM/PA if and when they are rehearsed in and applied to specific governmental/state contexts.

Table 1.1 Alleged differences of character and focus between public management and public administration

Public administration (PA)	Public management (PM)
Old-fashioned, traditional, introverted	Modern, outward-looking
Static hierarchies and procedures	Dynamic – leadership, innovation
Focus on following rules – compliance and accountability	Focus on managing resources – efficiency and performance
Focus on machinery of government	Focus on multi-stakeholder governance

1.3 Public management and public administration

You will have noticed from the title onwards that this book seems to be covering two subjects rather than one: public management and public administration. Let me say straight away that some scholars think there *are* two, but many others cannot see significant differences, and treat the field as one single academic community. I belong in the latter camp – the one that thinks there are no significant differences (for a succinct summary of this long-running argument, see Lynn, 2006, pp. 4–10). Those who claim that public management is different tend to point to one or more of the contrasts shown in Table 1.1.

Table 1.1 is written from the point of view of those PM scholars who see themselves as something newer and more dynamic than traditional PA. An early writer who thought that management was distinctive was the English half practitioner/half academic, Desmond Keeling. His 1972 book *Management in Government* was one of the more thoughtful explorations of what might be new about PM.

In the USA the PM/PA distinction has a particularly complex and intertwined history, going right back to the beginnings of the modern study of this field in the late nineteenth century. In the 1980s and 1990s American PM scholars saw PA as lacking in rigour and over-burdened with normative concerns. A group of PM academics set themselves up to escape from the perceived limitations of PA, so that they could more vigorously pursue high quality social science. Thus, at times various individual or group manifestos have stressed the differences between PM and PA, but one well-informed recent review concludes that nowadays almost all the topics and approaches used under one heading are also used under the other (Yang, 2015).

An opposite perspective from those who see PM as the "new thing" would be that of those PA scholars who claimed their own form of superiority. For much of the history of the subject in the USA many PA theorists there saw themselves as rather separate: "management" was primarily business-oriented and failed to appreciate the special organizational and normative complexities of government and politics, which were meat and drink to PA. PM was, in effect, merely a province of PA. On both sides of this argument there has been, perhaps, an element of academic boosterism (Raadschelders, 2011, p. 208).

In his review of the history of the issue in the USA Yang (2015) perceptively observes that:

> This considerable confusion is difficult to dismantle because the terms and their relationships are socially constructed by individuals possessing different values and assumptions. (Yang, 2015, p. 103)

So why do I resist these contrasts? For several reasons. First, I see the elements of Table 1.1 as somewhat stereotyped and false dichotomies. They do not match the real world. Anyone who believes that traditional public administrators were always introverted rule-followers with limited or no interest in leadership and innovation should settle down to read some administrative histories and biographies. For example, Daniel Carpenter's *The Forging of Bureaucratic Autonomy* (2001) depicts top administrators in US federal agencies as working actively to form supportive relationships with political groups and with the general public, seizing opportunities when they arose and carefully building the external legitimacy of their organizations. All this took place in the late nineteenth and early twentieth centuries. If we move into the second half of the twentieth century we may consider the autobiography of Roy Denman, a senior British official who served at the Board of Trade and the Cabinet Office before becoming a Director General in the European Commission (*The Mandarin's Tale*, Denman, 2002). He tells an exciting and amusing story in which senior officials were constantly inventing new strategems and trying (sometimes successfully, often unsuccessfully) to tell truth to power by explaining uncomfortable facts to reluctant or prejudiced ministers. Although operating in significantly different ways, the element of creativity was clearly central to many "bureaucratic" careers in the USA, the UK and the European Union (EU) institutions.

Neither (second) is a focus on the management of resources remotely a new thing for traditional administrators. Consider various publications written by Sir Richard (Otto) Clarke, a prominent English civil servant half a century or more ago. They are very much concerned with the strategic management of public expenditure and, within that, securing efficiency and effectiveness (for example, Clarke, 1972, 1978). These aspects of performance are not an exclusive preserve of something called management – they have very often been major foci for both theorists and practitioners in PA.

Third, while governance may have become a very popular concept among both academics and practitioners, and while it may have a useful core in recognizing that governments always govern with and along-side other powerful players, this set of circumstances is certainly not new to PA either. The public policy literature of the 1950s and 1960s was already full of debates about how different types of relationship between governments and pressure groups shaped the content and effectiveness of public policies. The theoretical frameworks may not have been exactly what they are now, but the basic idea that govern-ment was not some stand-alone, monolithic actor, but was embedded in webs of competing interests, was already established. "Hollowing out" (Rhodes, 1997) and the fashion for partnerships may have accen-tuated these features but in essence they are not new.

Fourth, while some may assert the existence of differences of style, focus or emphasis between *academic* PM and *academic* PA, I am not aware of any widely observed or accepted differences of academic theory or method. It is not as though certain theories or methods are the exclusive property of one group or the other. In other words, even if there may be some surface differences of image or emphasis, these do not seem to be reflected in the substance of academic work.

Fifth, in so far as we are still examining the academic world, there is no clear distinction between public *management* and public *administra-tion* in the nomenclature and practice of individual academics, their departments, their journals, their conferences or their research projects. Ironically, the adopted journal of the US Public *Management* Research Association (PMRA) is called the Journal of Public *Administration* Research and Theory (my italics). Speaking personally, I have been a professor in an American Department of *Public Administration*, an English Department of *Government*, a Dutch Department of *Public Administration* and a Belgian Institute of *Public Governance*. I did very similar work in all four, and published in journals which had both *management* and *administration* in their titles, all without a second thought. So did most of my colleagues.

There will be more about the nature of the public management community in Chapter 4, but that is probably enough for now on PM/PA differences, which I hope will not distract too many readers for too long. Please note, however, that from this point in the book I will usually use just the term "public management" (or "PM"), which should be understood as also covering the field of academic public administration (PA). "Public administration" will be retained in only a few particular circumstances where it would be awkward or artificial to change it.

1.4   Public management, private management, generic management?

It is already clear that PM as a field has rather vague and permeable borders. In the previous section we saw that some think there is a border between PM and PA, while others do not. There are also differences according to whether an Anglo-American "government" tradition or a continental "state" tradition is adopted (Rutgers, 2001). Now we can briefly examine another disputed frontier: that between public sector management and private sector management. To put the issue in the form of a question: Is PM different, or is it just part of the generic study of all management, public and private?

This and closely related questions have been long debated. Literally hundreds of articles and book chapters have been published dealing with some aspect (two summaries are Lynn, 2006, pp. 12–15 and Pollitt, 2003, pp. 1–25). Opinions range from the position that public and private management are alike in most important respects (here termed genericism) to the opposite pole, at which commentators argue that public management is fundamentally different. History does not give us very clear guidance, since almost every imaginable activity has at some time and place been both publically and privately conducted – including armies, breweries, hospitals, house-cleaning, railways, schools, tax collection and weather forecasting.

I do not have the space to climb this mountain of literature. Instead I will put forward my own interpretation which – largely though not entirely – coincides with that developed by the scholar who has probably made the deepest and most extensive study of this issue, the American professor Hal Rainey (see, for example, Rainey, 1997; Rainey and Bozeman, 2000).

A fundamental point is that the differences between public and private can be treated either descriptively, or normatively, or both. For some, the descriptive/analytical and the normative are intimately entangled, and inseparable. Thus some commentators, for example, are utterly convinced that the private sector is more efficient, and focus on examples of seemingly gross public sector inefficiency – but ignore the many examples of private sector inefficiency. They have a strong assumption or stereotype that influences their approach to evidence. Rainey and Bozeman (2000) refer to this as "the power of the *a priori*". Meanwhile, others believe that public sector staff are inherently more caring and more focused on the wider good of citizen and society than staff in the private sector. They too have little difficulty in finding cases – in this instance of private sector callousness and public sector caring. But, as in the previous example, they tend not to look very hard for cases of private sector caring, public spiritedness and generosity, or for cases where public service staff have treated their clients with a heartless lack of concern or courtesy. Both these last types of stereotype-breaking case are actually not that hard to find.

Now let us turn to the less normative, more empirical side of the literature. In Table 1.2 I have set out some of the dimensions of "publicness" identified and discussed in a classic work by Hal Rainey.

Table 1.2 is my adapted and simplified version of Rainey's original scheme. Even so, it remains quite complex, with a total of 16 characteristics where there may, or may not, be a significant difference between public sector and private sector management. Notice first that most of these are not black or white dichotomies, they are matters of degree. So, to take characteristic number 9, the goals of a public sector organization may be fairly vague, very vague or even non-existent.

So "publicness" begins to look like quite a complex idea – it may have 16 (or even more) dimensions, and most of these are matters of degree rather than either/or dichotomies. (Arguably more than 16, because it is easy to see that some of the lines in Table 1.2 could be further

Table 1.2 Distinctive characteristics of public management

ENVIRONMENTAL FACTORS

Not a market environment – revenue comes from a budget not from sales

Presence of elaborate formal legal constraints

Presence of intense political influences

ORGANIZATION/ENVIRONMENT TRANSACTIONS

Public organizations produce "public goods" in situations where there are large "externalities" (effects on others beyond those who directly consume the service)

Public services are often monopolistic and/or coercive

Public activities tend to have a broad impact in society, and often have high symbolic value

Public managers are subject to intense public scrutiny

Public managers are expected to display higher degrees of fairness, honesty, openess and accountability

ORGANIZATIONAL ROLES, STRUCTURES AND PROCESSES

Goals are often multiple, vague and conflicting; they may well be unmeasurable/ intangible

Lower decision-making autonomy and lower authority over subordinates

General management involves more political activity and more crisis management

More red tape, more organizational complexity, more processual requirements

Strategic decision-making more vulnerable to interventions by external groups

Fewer extrinsic incentives (such as high pay/benefits packages); weaker link between performance and pay

Public service ethos – more community/public interest-oriented work values

Greater caution/greater reluctance to innovate

Source: Extensively adapted from Rainey (1997, pp. 73–4).

subdivided, for example, line 5 or line 8.) Each dimension deserves a research programme of its own. Similarly, one must suppose that in private sector organizations there are also considerable variations. Some private sector managers work in jobs that directly confront them with relentless, cut-throat competition. Others work in much more sheltered jobs or organizations. Many private sector managers need have little to do with politicians or party politics, but some do – the chief executives of companies which are handling or bidding for big public contracts had better have their political antennae switched on. Equally, while top civil servants may be dealing with ministers on a daily basis, the clerical officer working in a stationery store probably does not feel any closer to the government and its ministers than an ordinary citizen. In short, a given organization may be more or less "public" in its various characteristics, with only a limited subset of all the many public sector agencies and ministries scoring as "purely" or "highly" public. What have been termed "hybrid" organizations are not at all unusual – indeed, many of the management reforms of the past quarter century (contracting out, partnerships and so on) have made them increasingly common. From this perspective, the borderline between public sector and private sector is not a line at all, but rather an extensive zone of hybridity. Many private sector organizations may contain elements of publicness, and many government agencies may contain elements usually associated with the private sector.

These complexities should make us cautious. Big generalizations about *either* the public *or* the private sector are likely to be confronted with numerous exceptions. But that does not rule out the possibility that there are "on average" types of difference of precisely the type listed in Table 1.1. Much – though not all – of the high quality empirical research seems to point in that general direction. So my conclusion is that there *are* significant differences, but that there is also a great deal of variation within each sector. One might also argue that the limited subset of organizations with highly public characteristics was a particularly powerful and important group, comprising departments of state, courts, national audit offices, the police and so on.

Incidentally, the complexities and variation alluded to above are one reason why the question of the relative efficiency of public and private sector organizations has never been conclusively settled. Although many commentators are convinced that the private sector is inherently more efficient, the scientific jury on this judgement is still out – and likely to remain so. There are so many methodological barriers to making a fair comparison. One would have to find reliable data over time that pertained to public and private organizations doing similar work under similar conditions. This is hard to do. But even if that is achieved, all that will have been proved is that, at that time, in respect of that particular activity, private sector organization A was more/less/equally efficient compared to public sector organization B. It still would not enable one to make confident generalizations about efficiency in the public sector as a whole or the private sector as a whole. Matters are not helped by the fact that, in many countries, the systems of national accounting do not make any allowance for changes in outputs and outcomes in public programmes, but focus on changes in inputs. This means that productivity gains in the public sector are not picked up, and that public and private sector accounting are conducted on dissimilar bases.

A different, though overlapping, approach to the public/private contrast comes from a pair of English academics who spent most of their academic lifetimes studying English local government (Ranson and Stewart, 1994). They tried to identify distinctive issues that public managers needed to give priority to a degree that most private sector managers did not. My interpretation of their conclusions are set out in Table 1.3.

Ranson and Stewart certainly had a normative element in their work. They were writing to try to safeguard the distinctiveness of the public sector at a time and place (the early 1990s in the UK) when they believed that distinctiveness was being eroded – with dangerous consequences. They wanted to highlight what they saw as the special qualities and commitments needed by public managers. I will make no further comment on this here, other than to say that if you are even partially convinced by their proposals, then it is worth noting that there are very similar challenges still around today. The fiscal austerity being experienced by public agencies in many European countries and in North America mean that pressures to "do more with less" are enormous. One – but only one – possible response to this is to cut back, contract out, tighten citizen eligibility for entitlements and generally make saving money *the* dominant value. Under such circumstances it is easy to begin to lose sight of some of the other public values advocated by Ranson and Stewart (and implicit in Rainey's list of public management characteristics).

What does this mean for the boundaries between the study of PM and the general (generic) study of management? My conclusion would be that PM can often learn from generic management, but always needs to reframe the findings of generic management studies in terms of the special characteristics which pertain (or, normatively, *should* pertain) in many parts of the public sector. Thus, running a corner grocery store probably will not have much to teach us about how best to run the UK Cabinet Office or the World Bank. Neither will research on human resource management policies for supermarket check-out staff easily translate into human resource management policies in a setting where public service motivation is likely to be

Table 1.3   Distinctive issues for public managers

DISTINCTIVE ISSUES FOR PUBLIC MANAGERS

Managing in a socio-political system. The need to understand the political process and work with elected politicians.

Working with public pressure and protest. These are necessary and healthy parts of the democratic process – normal, not exceptional.

A sense of accountability. The democratic context implies that openness needs to be not merely accepted, but actively promoted.

Understanding public behaviour. Citizens are not only customers, but also citizens, taxpayers and voters. This makes their relationships with public managers more complex and multi-dimensional than would be usual in a private sector commercial setting.

The management of rationing. Many public managers are in a position where they are obliged to ration – to say who comes first in the queue, who qualifies and who doesn't (for example, for hospital treatment, school places, social housing accomodation and so on). Rationing, while not unknown, is less common in commercial contexts, where the answer to excess demand is usually to make more of the product/service – and to increase profits.

The management of influence. Rather than competing with other organizations, public managers are frequently required to build partnerships and/or guide cooperative relationships.

Assessing multi-dimensional performance. The performance of public sector organizations can seldom be reduced to simple indicators such as "profit" or "efficiency". Public sector managers need to be able to construct and use more complex and multi-dimensional measures of performance and, indeed, sometimes to live with conflicting goals and targets (for example, speed up decisions on cases/make fewer mistakes).

Understanding a wider responsibility to a changing society. "[M]anaging in the public domain needs an understanding of societal change as necessary to a learning society" (Ranson and Stewart, 1994, p. 262).

Source: Derived and developed from the list of Ranson and Stewart (1994, pp. 261–2).

at a high level – such as a maternity unit in a public hospital or the secret service unit which guards the President of the United States (for public service motivation, see Perry and Hondeghem, 2008). On the other hand, studies of how most efficiently to purchase computers for a major corporation may have considerable resonance for computer purchase in a large government department. From time to time many governments have brought in successful businessmen and women to tackle perceived problems in public sector management. Some of these business people have had a measure of success, while others do not seem to have made any positive impact. It may well be that the more successful have been those who have best understood the subtlety and complexity of the relationships between public and private management.

This is not a purely empirical matter. There are also important normative issues here. If one wishes to promote particular sets of values as being specially appropriate to the public services, then organizational procedures and structures can be designed to encourage and support those values among staff. Most of us, I suspect, would wish the public servants who serve us to strive for high standards of integrity, impartiality, honesty, courtesy and so on. Most of us would like to believe that these staff had some consideration for the general welfare of us citizens, both collectively and individually. And, because it isn't a perfect world, we would also like to know that these staff could be held accountable for their actions, and that we citizens would have straightforward and effective procedures for complaining if we thought that we had been badly treated. All these desiderata need to be planned for, and continuously reinforced and monitored, rather than merely hoped for. They are therefore matters where public *management* is of crucial importance.

As a footnote, it should be noted that another permeable border is that between PM and public policy. The study of public policy as a named, distinct academic field grew rapidly in the 1960s and 1970s. At that time some academic staff migrated from departments of politics or public administration to departments or units of public policy. Policy analysis is also usually considered as one aspect of public policy studies, being particularly concerned with applied questions of how robust particular policies are or are likely to be, and by what decision processes policies and programmes were formulated and implemented. Policy analysis itself overlaps with policy and programme evaluation, which has become a considerable industry both in Europe and North America. As Riccucci notes (2010, pp. 33–6), public policy is another academic field with continuing identity problems and debates over contrasting theories and methods (Kay, 2006; Pawson, 2013). Thus policy studies/policy analysis/programme evaluation is a near neighbour of PM – a field with which PM often shares interests, and in whose journals PM scholars not infrequently report their research.

1.5   What kind of theories and methods are used in PM?

The short answer is that many kinds of theory and many kinds of method can be found in PM publications. There is no one dominant "school". The patterns of theory and method use are complex, and deserve more detailed treatment than can be afforded in this chapter. Therefore the whole of Chapter 2 will be devoted to theory, and Chapter 3 to methods. Most PM theories and methods, at least at the broad level, are not specific to PM but rather are part of the general repertoire of social science theories and techniques.

1.6   Where does academic PM come from?

The two most popular answers currently seem to be (a) the eighteenth-century German states and (b) eleventh-century China. Methods of administration were discussed in many early civilizations and regimes, including classical Greece and Rome and the Byzantine Empire (Lynn, 2006, pp. 40–54). Much later, there were also fascinating developments in early modern England, France, Germany and elsewhere. Thomas Cromwell, Henry VIII's humbly-born adviser and protagonist of the prize-winning novel and TV series *Wolf Hall* (Mantel, 2009) has been called "the first permanent secretary". He was the King's principal fixer from about 1533 until 1540, when Henry had him executed (history shows that Cromwell was not by any means the only top administrator to suffer such a fate, both in England and elsewhere). More than two hundred years later Napoleon created a formidable imperial bureaucracy, whose outlines are still visible in France today. And so on – every major European state could point to important administrative innovations and ideas during the period 1600–1900. What is less clear is how far the subject was studied in an academic way – as opposed to being discussed practically among administrators. This is a difficult question to answer, not simply because of the paucity of evidence, but also because of the danger of importing modern concepts ("independent study", "scientific", "university") into long past contexts where their meanings would have been quite different, or would not have applied at all.

One particularly interesting European forerunner of modern academic PM developed in the German states during the eighteenth century and involved, inter alia, the foundation of a series of university chairs in administrative studies (there were 23 of them by the end of that century). These chairs were closely involved in practical matters, as local (royal) rulers attempted to build up corps of trained civil servants, selected on a meritocratic basis. The emergence of this intertwining of practice and university-level study is known as cameralism, and it was notable for an attempt to develop rules and procedures that would realize and harmonize the interests of the ruler *and* the subjects. In some ways cameralism can be seen as an eighteenth-century precursor of the New Public Management (NPM) of the 1980s and 1990s (Hood and Jackson, 1991). In the German states this trend lost some of its distinctiveness as the nineteenth century progressed and, with ideas of the *Rechtsstaat* becoming increasingly influential, law became the "master discipline".

On the other hand, the eighteenth century looks positively recent if we pay attention to some of the historical work on Chinese administration. None of the European or North American states could claim to have had a major treatise on civil service organization written ten centuries ago (Wang Anshi's text *Wan Yan Shu* of 1058 – see Dreschler, 2013). Some Chinese enthusiasts go even further. Writing of China in the second century BC, one scholar claimed that:

> [A]n increasing number of officials was selected by civil service examinations . . . An increasing proportion of office holders were educated in an imperial university that was expressly founded, in 124 BC, for the purpose of inculcating in future officials the values and attitudes desired by the government. (Creel, 1964, pp. 155–6, cited in Lynn, 2006, p. 41)

Again, caution is necessary here. While there are now a number of interpretations of early Chinese administrative thought available in western publications, these are sometimes disputed by Chinese scholars (for example, see Ma et al., 2015). However, whatever meanings may be placed upon Wang Anshi and other forefathers, the sheer antiquity of the ideas remains impressive.

The more recent history of academic PM is clearer. It would be only a small exaggeration to say that each state, or group of states, has its own history of leading ideas and figures. Studying in the UK I was anointed with Bentham, J.S. Mill, nineteenth-century arguments about whether public organizations should be headed by boards or individuals and the great Northcote Trevelyan civil service reforms which began in the mid 1850s. Then nothing much seemed to happen until the huge growth of the welfare state after the Second World War (this apparent half century wasteland was an illusion, but either I did not study hard enough or my teachers were not interested in that period!).

Had I been American it would likely have been Woodrow Wilson, Frederick Winslow Taylor, scientific management and the "progressive" movement. (Lenin, incidentally, was a considerable admirer of scientific management!) Also my studies would probably have taken in John Dewey and John Gaus, then Roosevelt's "New Deal" and the 1937 Brownlow Report, plus, of course, the uniqueness of the American democratic context. I would almost certainly have been taught about the great post Second World War arguments between the two father figures of modern US PM thought, Herbert Simon and Dwight Waldo (in fact some less ambitious US curricula might even have started here – see Van Thiel, 2014, pp. 9–13).

Had I been German, cameralism would have featured, no doubt followed by Von Stein (a far-sighted Head of the Prussian civil service). The story of the gradual establishment of the theory and practice of the *Rechtsstaat* would have brought me into intimate contact with the role and importance of the law in public administration. In the early twentieth century I could hardly have avoided the towering figure of Max Weber, whose elaboration of an "ideal type" of bureaucracy is still foundational to the field of PM, both in Germany and globally.

And if I had been a French student I would have studied Vauban, Louis XIV's great administrator, and I certainly could not have escaped Napoleon and the founding of the *grand corps* in the early nineteenth century. No doubt I would also have encountered Charles-Jean Bonnin's 68 administrative principles from 1812. I would have seen how the status and power of the top officials grew, even as the French party political system suffered regular weakness and failure. "In France constitutions come and go, but administrative institutions remain" (Rohr, 2002, p. 18). Then in the first half of the twentieth century Henri Fayol was a leading French name in management theory, and in the second half Michel Crozier became internationally famous for his analyses of bureaucracy.

Understandably, only a few brave scholars have attempted to command this range of sources and languages. The diversity reflects the fact that, until comparatively recently, public administration, both practically and academically, was an overwhelmingly domestic/nationally circumscribed topic. In many cases, including my own, teaching in PM would not have strayed far beyond the story of one's own country, its leading thinkers and principal reformers. Behind these national stories, however, there was actually a good deal of international exchange of ideas. For example, the scientific management ideas of Frederick Winslow Taylor travelled to a number of European countries, while Henri Fayol's theory of management travelled back across the Atlantic in the opposite direction. Lynn (2006) gives a good short account of these mutual, international influences.

Since the 1970s the level of intellectual parochialism in PM has declined. The market for PM ideas and techniques has become more obviously international, as have the flows of postgraduate students and researchers. International consultancies operate in many countries, and organizations like the OECD and the World Bank have proven influential in setting reform agendas and spreading ideas of "best practice".

1.7 What is PM about?

What are the topics and themes which PM scholars inquire into and write about? The answer changes over *time*, but there is also great variation in *level* at which questions are asked and studies are conducted. By level here I mean how broad the topic is. Thus, at the "large" end, PM scholars may ask what have been the broad trends of public management reform across different countries and continents (Pollitt and Bouckaert, 2011). Meantime, at the "small" end, other scholars may focus on exactly how Accident and Emergency (A&E) patient waiting times are measured in six local hospitals (a friend of mine once discovered that the waiting times were measured in substantially different ways in different hospitals, which meant that the national statistics ranking hospitals on how quick they were at seeing A&E patients were unreliable). Since the object of study is government – or governance – the range of possible topics is huge. Opening some recent journal issues I found the following among their articles (these are my simplified versions of the original titles):

- street-level policy entrepreneurship
- the effect of the government's use of social media on the reliability of government
- do NPM-type reforms lead to a cultural revolution within public sector organizations?

- collaborative network capacity
- service quality, administrative process and citizens' evaluation of local government
- the transformation of Swiss federal elites
- what is ahead for the senior civil service in Greece
- the search for identity in public administration
- the ability to face threats of cyberterrorism
- public service motivation (PSM)
- reasons for the lack of implementation of healthcare reforms in China
- experiments in public management research.

This opportunity sample is certainly varied. The underlying issues are somewhat less so. Thus fundamentals such as (inter alia) accountability, organizational form (hierarchies, networks and so on), performance, cultural change, external pressures and citizen participation crop up in many places and at several different levels.

In the ongoing flux of PM academic fashion, certain topics rise and others fall. Since the mid 1990s governance, complexity, networks, leadership, performance management, corruption, co-production and transparency have all been rising themes. Meanwhile interest in other, formerly prominent, topics seems to have dwindled. Examples would be formal organizational structures, planning (which in so far as it survives as a focus of interest seems to involve urban geographers rather than PM specialists) and (curiously, given the current austerity) budgetary processes. Administrative history also seems to have shrunken somewhat as a subfield. This is not to say that nobody studies these formerly popular topics anymore, but simply that the work of the few that do seldom feature in the leading journals, and the topics themselves tend no longer to form the headline themes for major international conferences. We will say more about these cycles and waves of academic fashion when the PM academic community is described in Chapter 4.

A few scholars have undertaken the gargantuan task of trying systematically to map what the topics of academic PM are. Readers who wish to probe this conceptual cartography in more detail are recommended to begin with Raadschelders (2011, pp. 103–26).

I conclude this section on a lighter note. In the Preface I mentioned the difficulty there could be when one was asked what one was studying.

How could one craft a concise answer that was intelligible to a questioner who knew nothing about the field? When an American friend of mine – an accomplished PM professor – read a draft of this chapter he emailed me as follows: "My answer to the question has evolved into: 'I specialize in government programs that get screwed up – so I never run out of work or have to worry about tenure.'" As a comparativist, I would just add that this kind of joke is probably more common in the USA and the UK than in, say, Finland or Germany. In the former pair of countries the image of government as constantly prone to error is culturally more prevalent than in the latter (though that says nothing about what the underlying rate of "real" errors may be).

1.8   Why study it?

This seemingly fundamental question is surprisingly seldom asked. The answer – whatever it might be – is taken for granted: if you have signed up for the course then let's get on with the curriculum! Furthermore, there seem to be few sources of empirical information about such motives. One unusual attempt was *Perspectives for the Future*, a collection in which European PM scholars were asked about why they were working in the field and what impacts they hoped their work would have (Bouckaert and Van de Donk, 2010). Interestingly, a number of the professors who gave their personal histories for that volume appeared to have come into the field almost by accident. I was one such myself, in that I had first become a civil servant and then later thought that a short spell in a university – researching the Whitehall world I had been working in – would be useful. So I made arrangements to become an academic for three years, and then return to the civil service. I had not foreseen that I would become so involved in university life that I would never return to my Whitehall desk. But I did discover many academic colleagues who, like me, had started their careers in the public sector – as social workers or local government officers or civil servants. Other colleagues had migrated from other parts of academia – for example, from engineering, physics and the law.

What was clear, however, was that many of them (us) in one sense or another wanted to "do good". They (we) saw the possibility of improving services to citizens, or democratic decision-making, or the implementation of major public programmes, or the administration of justice, as both personally and collectively important. This is a partly practical, partly ethical and motivational commitment. In my experience those who do not share in this at all are probably a minority among PM academics. It is not surprising that one of the booming topics of the past three decades in PM has been public service motivation (PSM – see Perry et al., 2010). This is the idea that those who work in the public services tend to be more altruistic and pro-social in their values and attitudes than those who work in the market sector. My point here would be that this concept can be applied to PM academics as well as PM practitioners. Consider the first words in one of the key works on PSM: "We undertook this book on motivation in public management because we are deeply committed to values of the academy and public service" (Perry and Hondeghem, 2008, p. vii).

Alongside this normative purpose lies the intrinsic fascination of finding out how things are done, administratively and managerially speaking. Just as some people like looking under the bonnet of a car, PM academics often want to look under the bonnets/hoods of government and public agencies. When presidents or ministers decide that they want to create equal access to education, or to stimulate investment in an economically backward region, or to reduce crime, just exactly how is the problem translated into actual resources, staff, organizations and procedures? How can equality of citizen access be guaranteed in practice? How is it possible to hold big, powerful bureaucracies accountable, and to make them transparent? Why do some public programmes work quite well and others fail?

Paradoxically, one of the policies where the identification of outcomes has been most difficult (and neglected) has been the policy of public management reform itself (Pollitt, 2013b). A painstaking evaluation of the myriad public management reforms in UK central government between 1979 and 2010 came to the conclusion that running costs actually increased, and public complaints soared. But during the research it also became clear that relevant data over time were very hard to pin down, partly because ministers and civil servants did not seem to be very interested in monitoring the outcomes of their own promises and commitments (Hood and Dixon, 2015).

Another set of questions relate to bigger and more dramatic issues. If our societies and their governing institutions are to preserve some kind of welfare state through the current phase of fiscal austerity, then the better management of public programmes and services will almost certainly play a crucial role. And climate change poses even more widespread and severe threats, against which public authorities will be key players in a multitude of different ways. These "megatrends" are discussed further in Chapter 6, and they provide powerful rationales for the study of PM.

Nestling within these particular questions there are other, more general questions that engage PM scholars. For example, are there *general* conditions that underpin all or most successful programmes? Are there forms of organizations which usually seem to be more efficient or effective than other forms of organization – at least for specific types of programme? One outstanding PM scholar began his publishing career with a book that posed the fundamental question of whether there are general limits to administration (Hood, 1976). Are there some kinds of issue which cannot be "solved" administratively? Or, to put it in a different way, does all public administration entail deep and unavoidable trade-offs, which politicians are unwilling to admit to, but administrators and managers know only too well? This latter thought has exercised many leading scholars, some of whom have identified these trades-offs, each of which tends to give rise to contradictory pairs of proverbs or maxims for action (Hood and Jackson, 1991; Pollitt and Bouckaert, 2011; Simon, 1946).

So there are several principal motivations for studying the field of PM, ranging from pure intellectual curiosity about how organizational processes work, through high theory concerning the limits to our collective efforts to manage public affairs, on to some very practical concerns about improving daily administration, then to global challenges to our welfare and security and, finally, to deeply felt convictions that the public sphere should be one characterized by high moral values and ethical standards.

1.9   Key reading

In this chapter, and throughout the remainder of the book, many recommendations for further reading on specific issues are given in the text. Here at the end of this chapter a few more general recommendations are in order.

The two best-known recent introductions to the subject are both American. In 2010 Norma Riccucci published *Public Administration: Traditions of Inquiry and Philosophies of Knowledge* and the following year Jos Raadschelders produced *Public Administration: The*

Interdisciplinary Study of Government. Both are well worth reading – not only in relation to this chapter but for the next two chapters as well. Raadschelders's book is longer and goes into greater scholarly detail. If you like typologies and conceptual diagrams, this will engage you. Both books share the general thrust of my first chapter, at least in the sense that both recognize the multi-disciplinary nature of PM, see it as potentially a strength and are critical of those voices which have asserted that one particular theory or method should be dominant, or should be regarded as the "real" PM. Both are slightly Americo-centric – though by no means as much as other US texts.

More space to European concerns is given in Larry Lynn's lively, short book *Public Management: Old and New* (2006). This offers an excellent potted history of PM ideas in France, Germany, the UK and the USA. Larry was also author of a chapter entitled "Public management: a concise history of the field" in the 2005 *Oxford Handbook of Public Management* (Ferlie et al., 2005). For those with large appetites (it runs to 789 pages) this handbook will provide much general sustinence. One chapter which has particular relevance here is Hal Rainey and Young Han Chun's "Public and private management compared" (pp. 72–102).

One older book which has never been bettered is Andrew Dunsire's history of administrative ideas, *Administration: The Word and the Science* (1973). Many university libraries still have copies.

Finally, an accessible/informal treatment can be found in my 2003 book *The Essential Public Manager.* It covers such topics as the differences between public and private management, fashions in management thought and the getting and giving of PM advice.

1.10   The layout of the rest of the book

The next two chapters deal with theory (Chapter 2) and methods and approaches (Chapter 3). Any introduction to an academic subject, advanced or not, has to address these two sets of issues. In the case of PM these two chapters necessarily embrace some of the most vivid debates in the field. PM academics love to argue among themselves about theories and methods. No one book could offer a comprehensive guide to these ongoing debates, but Chapters 2 and 3 provide a preliminary orientation. Chapter 4 introduces a more anthropological perspective on the community of PM academics themselves. Who are they, where do they operate, how do they assess themselves, what do they actually do? One of the things that many PM scholars spend a lot of time on is working for or with practitioners. This relationship with the world of practice has played a central role in the development of the academic field, and in Chapter 5 it is examined in some depth. The following Chapter 6 is also concerned with the external world, but from another perspective altogether. It looks at major trends in the external environment which carry big implications for the future study and practice of PM. It also identifies what seem to be the topical trends within the academic community, and reflects on the relation between these impulses within academia and the likely pressures from outside. The final, short Chapter 7 tries to imagine some possible futures for the subject.

On a practical note, this is not a book of equal chapters. The next two – theory (Chapter 2) and methods (Chapter 3) – are considerably longer than the others. That is because they have more ground to cover. If you are reading with a time budget you should therefore count Chapters 2 and 3 as virtually double length units.

2 Theory

"Theory" can mean very different things to different people. (Robson, 2002, p. 61)

The study of public administration is probably further away than ever from reaching a theoretical closure to its identity crisis. (Raadschelders, 2011, p. 126)

2.1 Foreword: ontologies and epistemologies

Before diving into theory there is a need to carry out a small amount of terminological ground-clearing. In this short section I will discuss the ontologies and epistemologies underlying the academic study of PM. What I mean by these words is as follows:

Ontology: assumptions about the nature of reality or, more precisely, the nature of the phenomena which the researchers wish to study. What exists "out there", and what exists "in here" (in our minds) and what is the relationship between them? Some believe that we can directly perceive and test an externally existing reality (positivists), while others suggest that we more or less extensively create that external reality within our own minds (constructivists or interpretivists).

Epistemology: how can claims to knowledge be justified? This embraces issues of how "knowledge" is defined, what criteria should govern its creation, what are its sources and, ultimately, what kinds of knowledge are possible (or impossible). It includes questions of to what extent "objectivity" is possible, how far "subjectivity" is inevitable and whether some kinds of objectivity or subjectivity are in some senses better than others.

In respect of both ontology and epistemology PM is one of many fields where much more general debates (sometimes wars) rage (see, for example, Raadschelders, 2011; Whetsell and Shields, 2015). These debates sometimes take new turns, but in essence they go back a very long way – usually to classical Greek philosophy.

Anyone hoping for a distinct set of theories labelled "public management" is in for a big disappointment. While there are certain middle and low level theories which are specific to the governmental subject matter of PM, most of the big theories (and their attendant controversies) are imported from the social sciences more generally. There is nothing wrong with this, indeed it is one sign that PM is a paid-up member of the broader social scientific community.

2.2 The plan of the chapter

The strategy of this chapter is as follows. First, there is a brief discussion of the importance of theory. Second, there is a sequence of sections dealing with particular theories. I have been obliged to make selections, and some commentators will undoubtedly believe that I have unjustifiably left their pet theory out. Regrettably, this cannot be helped (indeed, I have even left some of my own pet theories out). The full range of theories used by PM scholars is so broad that a whole book could scarcely do justice to them. I have tried to choose theories which are in widespread current use within the PM academic community. I have also included brief examples of their application. In this way, I can at least give a flavour of how theories are used in mainstream PM, and what some of the controversies are about. Third, after the treatment of particular theories, I discuss two elements which frame and pervade the use of theory: time and specific contextual features which characterize particular countries, sectors or organizations. When in use most – though not all – theories are frequently said to need to be set in time or context, and it is worth taking a look at what might be meant by this. At the end of the chapter I suggest some key reading. This chapter and the next one (methods) are the longest in the book, because they have so much ground to cover.

2.3 Theory, concepts and description: why theory is so important, but not all important

A frequent criticism heard from professors as they assess PM theses, articles and books runs as follows: "It was too descriptive. Not enough theory." This comment is widely accepted, but the assumptions underlying it are often not discussed. Before going any further, I would like to explore the description/theory distinction a little further.

The most important underlying assumptions are twofold. First, that the *real* job of PM scholars (or, more broadly, social scientists) is to produce explanations. Second, that (mere) descriptions are not explanations, because to explain one has to have a theory. A theory is a device which will tell you not simply *what* happened (description) but *why* it happened (explanation).

My own view is that in everyday academic life these distinctions are nowhere near as sharp as they are often taken to be, and that we must also recognize that what different authorities mean by "explanation" itself varies. Even if we take a position that says a description is not a proper explanation, that does not mean that good description is not worth doing. Good description is of enormous value in itself. Imagine yourself listening to an explanation of why the police had failed to capture a fleeing terrorist if you had no prior descriptive knowledge of what the police were, what their powers and functions were supposed to be or how they were organized.

But descriptions can go further than that – they can do more than simply providing some kind of factual foundation on which explanatory theories can be built. A detailed description of the procedures of the UK House of Commons may explain *why* the government could not get a particular bill through to legislation. It came up against procedural barriers and there was not time for it to get through all its stages before Parliament was dissolved because of a forthcoming general election. This isn't a fancy theory with an impressive name, it is a description of what procedures hold under given circumstances, but it nevertheless delivers a perfectly servicable explanation.

It all depends what one means by "explanation". As mentioned, one mainstream view is that an explanation must answer the question of why something did or did not happen. It must identify a cause or causes that is/are necessary and sufficient to account for the phenomenon or outcome under study. However, this does not end the debate. Even among mainstream social scientists there are significantly different concepts of causation. We do not have time (or competence!) to go through the extensive philosophical debates here, but Kurki (2008) provides a useful summary of them, in which she identifies at least four principal candidates: material causes; formal causes; efficient causes; and final causes (yes, these go back to Aristotle, although they are formulated differently in the twenty-first century). These are not stark alternatives but can be used in various combinations. Beyond this, however, some post-modernist theorists effectively reject the whole concept of explanation, or at least the concept of "causes", refusing to privilege any one set of subjective understandings or interpretations over any other (Bogason, 2005).

However, even if we put the post-modernists to one side (though see Section 2.13) and stay within the realms of orthodox social science there are still significant variations in the ways in which "theory" is conceived and formulated. For some a theory is a formal statement of one or more causal relationships in a real world, either deterministic or probabilistic. From the broad formal statement a number of more precise hypotheses can be derived and tested. These hypotheses can be shown to be true or false and, if false, the theory must be adjusted and one or more new hypotheses put forward. This is not too far from the traditional model of the natural sciences. It is variously known as "positivism" or a "deductive" approach (Van Thiel, 2014; Whetsell and Shields, 2015). For example, in a recent article on tax collection in Colombia, the authors put forward a total of seven hypotheses, one of which was that: "Governmental transparency is positively associated with property tax collection" (Petrovsky and Avellaneda, 2014, p. 151). The authors conducted a quantitative analysis in which, inter alia, they investigated the correlations between property tax collected as a percentage of total property valuation and a province-based transparency index combining indicators of visibility, oversight and institutionalisation. The findings of this analysis included the existence of a positive (but rather weak) association between the transparency index and the property tax collected. The highest aspiration of this species of deductive theorizing is to find general regularities in relationships – correlations which hold across many times and places, and thus begin to look like a general law. Unfortunately – and not for want of effort – not many such general and invariant relationships have yet been found, at least not in PM.

For other scholars, however, the form of the theory does not need to be so "fixed" (Robson, 2002, pp. 4–5). Instead theory can indicate that in a general way there is a strong relationship between certain factors, without crystallizing these into detailed hypotheses. Thus, for example, the civil service culture in Germany can be said to be generally more legalistic than in the UK and this can then be used as a reason for why certain types of reform may be more difficult to implement in Germany than the UK. Nor is it by any means always seen as essential for theories and hypotheses to be predictive. Explanations are also conceived as plausible sets of reasons why something happened in the past, that is, they are hindsighted (Kay, 2006, pp. 22–4). Thus, for example, one might argue that since the 1960s, the departments in UK central government have been restructured far more often than the departments of state in the USA because it is legally and procedurally much easier to make such structural changes in the UK, and because the UK government is far stronger vis-à-vis the legislature than the USA. This explanation refers to the past and does not take the form of a precise hypothesis. It is inductive and interpretive rather than deductive (Van Thiel, 2014). The implication is that it is likely to hold in the future, but only as far as the two key conditions hold. Neither is it part of some more general theory (although perhaps it could be built up towards one). It refers to the UK and the USA, and does not make any claim about how things are in Germany, France or liberal democracies in general.

Somewhere in between theory and description lies the zone of building taxonomies and conceptual models. Some PM scholars regard this kind of activity as "theory building", but others do not. A conceptual scheme cannot by itself answer a "why?" question, even if concepts are vital ingredients of theories (for example, you cannot have a theory of how to increase the efficiency of a healthcare system without using some concept of efficiency). PM seems to be a field in which the construction, amendment and elaboration of conceptual schemes has become a major occupation. Leading PM journals often feature articles which are concerned with refining big concepts such as accountability, governance or transparency. On the one hand, this is important work *if* it contributes to better theories. On the other, there is the danger that some scholars tend to get bogged down in ever finer conceptual distinctions, without contributing much either to theory or empirical research (Pollitt and Hupe, 2011). Over-elaborate conceptual schemes may make it more rather than less difficult to carry out empirical research, and can also help to reduce the accessibility of PM academic texts to practitioners.

None of this is intended as a diminution of the importance of theory. Theory remains at the heart of what PM scholars are doing and should be trying to do. Explanation *is* very important and theories *are* the principal vehicles for explanation. So theories are vital. At the same time, however, (a) there is no general agreement on exactly what constitutes causal explanation; (b) good description is not to be disparaged – it is extremely valuable; (c) the borders between describing and explaining are ambiguous and permeable; and (d) the form of a conventional theoretical explanation can vary from a very formal and precise set of statements to a looser description of a broad set of probabilistic relationships which are expected to hold in some but not all circumstances.

2.4 "Big name" theories

Since I cannot cover all the theories which PM scholars use, I must select. In the subsequent sections I give bare-bones accounts of three bodies of theory which are well known and widely applied within our field. I term these "big name" theories. They are (a) neo-institutionalism; (b) rational choice theory; and (c) governance theory. Each of these could better be described as a family of theories rather than a simple, singular idea. There are variations within each, which means that attacking just a few features of them is likely to misrepresent and underestimate the overall contribution which they can make. What is more, these big name theories never stand still. Central to the academic process is constant modification and elaboration, as scholars seek to explain inconsistencies, clarify apparent ambiguities and add supplementary arguments. So we are dealing with "moving targets". There is no absolute solution to this problem, although I have tried to (a) stay fairly general (rather than get bogged down in the finer points, which also have the highest rate of change) and (b) focus on the core ideas (which cannot change too much, or the theory itself becomes a different one). Nevertheless, readers should regard this chapter as no more than a taster – something which gives an introductory flavour of PM theorizing.

None of these theories is unique to PM. All are widely used in other fields of the social sciences. Neo-institutionalism has a sociological and political science pedigree. Rational choice theory developed in economics and political science. Governance theory also comes from political science. Even so, some of the most interesting applications of these theories have taken place within PM.

A final preliminary observation would be that, in broad terms, two kinds of theory discussion can be found on the pages of PM books and journals. One type is fairly abstract and concerns the concepts and proposed logical connections between them. Thus critics may point out that a given theory contains conceptual ambiguities and/or what appear to be logical contradictions. The other type is more concrete and practical, and concerns the challenges of *applying* a given theory to a given administrative system, case or set of data. Although a particular theory may be elegant and intellectually satisfying that does not not necessarily mean that it will be easy to apply if one wishes to explain, say, changes in the morale of municipal refuse collection workers in Hamburg. Perhaps their fall in morale was because of a changed employment contract, or the arrival of a new, abrasive boss, or the refusal of the municipality to replace their ageing fleet of vehicles, or a less cooperative, more complaining general public, or a general economic downturn in Germany? Or perhaps it was a reversion to the normal level of morale after a previous but exceptional year during which there had been a large wage increase and Hamburg refuse collection had won an international public service quality award? Or it could be any combination of these factors. How does one apply a theory to this set of multi-dimensional, combinatorial possibilities? In what follows I have tried, however briefly, to address both issues of pure theory and issues of making theories work in practice.

2.5   Some big name theories: 1. neo-institutionalism

Institutionalism begins with the institution (or organization – we will come to that in a moment) rather than the individual. The prime focus is on how institutions work, and how they shape both the choices and the norms and beliefs of the individuals who work within them. Institutionalists usually believe that the influence of the institution on the individual employee is extensive. An institution will have its own culture ("the way we think about things around here"), norms ("we always stand up for each other") and values ("caring for patients comes before saving money"). It can be hard for an individual to stand out against these collectively accepted precepts. There may be a dominant "logic of appropriateness" which says "in these circumstances what we do in this organization is X, Y, Z". Such a logic may often take precedence over the "logic of consequences" ("if I do this then that will probably happen"). At the extreme, soldiers may knowingly go to almost certain death for the honour of their country or regiment, and/ or for the sake of their fellow soldiers. They do what seems appropriate, even if the consequence is death or injury.

The term "neo-institutionalism" is commonly used to distinguish scholarly work since the early 1980s from the earlier, or traditional institutionalism. In traditional institutionalism comparisons were made of formal institutions – constitutions, parliaments, civil services, systems of justice and so on – but these tended to be rather static and taxonomic. Thus one had Westminster systems, presidential systems, unitary states, federal states and so on. Traditional institutionalism also had quite a strong legalistic/constitutional thread. Organizations were often classified and analysed according to their legal status.

What was new about the new institutionalism was partly that it arose in a changed academic world, where the study of politics and public administration had become more focused on individual behaviour and the play of conflicting interests, and traditional institutionalism had become looked down upon as old-fashioned. A foundational text of the new institutionalism, *Rediscovering Institutions*, began with a long critique of the then dominant theories of politics, which, it claimed, were reductionist, instrumentalist and individualist:

> Outcomes at the system level are thought to be determined by the interactions of individuals acting consistently in terms of the axioms of individual behavior, whatever they may be. Thus, we make assumptions about individual consumers to understand markets, about voters to understand politics, and about bureaucrats to understand bureaucracies. (March aand Olsen, 1989, p. 5)

Against this approach, March and Olsen wanted to rediscover the organization as an active force in politics and PM. They argued that:

> Bureaucratic agencies, legislative committees, and appellate courts are arenas for contending forces, but they are also collections of standard operating procedures and structures that define and defend values, norms, interest, identities, and beliefs. (March and Olsen, 1989, p. 17)

Notice that here institutions are not so much being defined by their legal status and formal powers but by their procedures and their influence in shaping values, norms and even identities.

Later in the book the authors explain how institutions can affect individuals:

When individuals enter an institution, they try to discover, and are taught, the rules. When they encounter a new situation, they try to associate it with a situation for which rules already exist. Through rules and a logic of appropriateness, political institutions realize both order, stability and predictability, on the one hand, and flexibility and adaptiveness on the other.

A logic of appropriateness can be contrasted with a logic of consequentiality. In a logic of consequentiality, behaviors are driven by preferences and expectations about consequences. (March and Olsen, 1989, p. 160)

This is an approach which consciously stands against the idea that politics and PM can be successfully analysed in terms of rationally calculated individual behaviours. It does not deny the importance of individual decisions, but sees those decisions as being taken within strongly influential organizational contexts. Powerful organizations can themselves be viewed as a sort of actor, they argue, and they play an important role in shaping the norms and values of their members. Most decisions within such organizations are driven by the desire to act appropriately rather than by the desire to achieve some consequence of personal importance to the individual actor.

It is important to ask what is an institution – how is it defined? There is no single, agreed and shared answer to this. (In fact there are so many varieties of neo-institutionalism and accompanying definitions of institutions that, even at book length, Peters (2000) occasionally confesses that he lacks the space to spell out all the details. Here I am obliged to be even more brutal.) March and Olsen do not provide a tight, easily operationalizable definition. In fact they actually offer slightly different versions in different parts of their work. They describe institutions as "collections of interrelated rules and routines that define appropriate action in terms of relations between roles and situations" (March and Olsen, 1989, pp. 21–6). Institutions are durable over time and have the capacity to shape the behaviour of their members. They are therefore strongly normative in both essence and effect. Another definition is that institutions are "the formal rules, compliance procedures, and standard operating procedures that structure the relationships between people in various units of the polity and economy" (Hall, 1986, p. 7). As critics have pointed out, these and other institutionalist definitions carry with them problems. To begin with, they are not at all easy to operationalize for empirical research. They tend to be large and abstract. Also, they often fail to distinguish between institutions and organizations. Yet that distinction can be important: the legal system and the medical profession are institutions (in the senses given above) but a court and a hospital are organizations. In a good deal of PM scholarship neo-institutionalist theories are applied to specific organizations or groups of organizations.

We have already glanced at the work of March and Olsen (which Peters labels "normative institutionalism"). From the menu of other institutionalisms two more are now selected for short depictions – "historical institutionalism" and "sociological institutionalism". Historical institutionalists have been deeply concerned with the question of how institutions develop (or stagnate) over time. Some public sector organizations are remarkably durable, surviving many changes of government and policy. Institutionalists have attempted to explain this durability, using concepts such as path dependency, layering and displacement (Pollitt, 2008, pp. 40–59; Streeck and Thelen, 2005). In path dependency a situation exists where there are one or more positive feedback mechanisms – that is, actors are rewarded for going further down the existing path rather than trying to begin different paths (Pierson, 2004). For example, political rewards within a first past the post, majoritarian electoral system such as in the UK usually go to those who exaggerate their own party's distinctiveness and relentlessly attack the credibility and motives of their opponents. Those who, by contrast, advocate cooperation and coalition, are not rewarded by such a system. Yet at the same time, in electoral systems with proportional representation, multiple parties and tendency to coalition government (such as Finland) cooperative behaviour is expected and even praised, while UK-type "attack dog" behaviour represents a departure from the path and is regarded as "bad form".

However, the existence of strongly self-reinforcing paths does not mean that no change at all can occur. Streeck and Thelen (2005) and others have refined the theory so as to allow for various kinds of more gradual change, such as "layering" (where new institutions are deposited on top of the old ones, instead of replacing them) or "displacement" (where an existing institution gradually takes on new purposes – such as a national audit office which had previously focused on traditional financial audit branching off into performance audit and evaluation). There is a rich sub-literature detailing different types of process by which gradual, incremental changes can come about.

But historical institutionalists have also been fascinated by the occasions when paths break, and sudden changes do take place (often termed "punctuations" in the literature). These are envisaged as "windows of opportunity", when three usually seperate streams of elements come together – problems, policies and political activity (Kingdon, 1995). Policy entrepreneurs are sometimes able to sense/see these conjunctions, and use them to facilitate radical change. The ideas or policies behind radical change may have been around for some time, but they have hitherto lacked problems to provoke action and politicians who can see advantage in taking that action. Such windows do not guarantee success, but in their absence big, sudden change is even harder to implement, or even see the possibility of.

Sociological institutionalism has provided the basis for a number of PM studies. Particularly influential have been the ideas of institutional isomorphism (Di Maggio and Powell, 1983; Meyer and Rowan, 1977). Organizations in the same field are often found to adopt similar structures and techniques – to become more and more alike (isomorphic). Thus fashions can sweep through whole public sectors (for creating semi-autonomous agencies, or central strategy units, or for employing techniques such as Total Quality Management). It might be thought that these isomorphic processes are driven by functional considerations – that the new forms and techniques are more efficient or economical. However, the sociological institutionalists argue that functional superiority is seldom demonstrated, and that a better explanation is the search for legitimacy. Organizations face uncertain environments and demands for change. One way of dealing with this is to adopt (even if only in name) a reform which is said to have been successful elsewhere – preferably with some high status organization in the same organizational field. Sometimes these acts of copying may be imposed from above (central government insists that particular groups of public sector organizations shall all have performance budgets or shall contract out certain services), in which case we can speak of "coercive isomorphism". At other times forms may spread through professional networks or other authoritative associations – "normative isomorphism". This can occur through procedures of licensing and accreditation, or less formally. But very often it is simply the desire to secure organizational legitimacy which best explains the copying of allegedly successful forms from other organizations ("mimetic isomorphism").

Neo-institutionalism is a broad church, and has the advantage that it directly addresses the nature of the organizations which populate the public sector. It can be fruitful in comparative work because it immediately directs attention to differences in the basic institutional frameworks in different countries – and these differences do indeed seem to be both influential and durable (Lynn, 2006; Pollitt and Bouckaert, 2009, 2011). The picture it paints of institutions as both shaping and being shaped by individual actors rings true with everyday experience. The logic of appropriateness is a powerful and persuasive idea that does seem to apply in many familiar situations. In its historical version institutionalism presents a way of getting beyond snapshots and cross-sectional studies of public sector organizations and into the patterns of evolution over time – trajectories that may be remarkably stable or sharply punctuated, and which may reveal public sector organizations not as simple types of this or that but rather as layered, like a sedimentary geological formation, with different aspects of culture and structure surviving alongside or on top of each other from different periods of time.

Yet the limitations of neo-institutionalism are equally apparent. To begin with, the definition of "institution" is neither precise nor universally held. Furthermore, this is not a body of theory that tends to produce neat, falsifiable hypotheses. It posits rather looser, more general connections between institutional cultures, standard operating procedures, and specific processes and decisions. Some commentators have claimed that these relationships are too vague and can never be falsified.

Finally, I offer a brief account of two cases of neo-institutionalism in action. The first is from a book I wrote with a colleague which looked at developments in the Belgian and UK hospital systems, and the Belgian and UK police forces, over the period from 1965 to 2005 (Pollitt and Bouckaert, 2009). We used a historical institutionalist perspective, and focused on how, and how much, the management of these two major public services had changed over the four decades under study. We looked in some detail at two particular localities but also at the shifting frameworks of national policies. We interviewed key figures, consulted documentary records, searched for data on the performance of the different systems and spent a good deal of time in the localities concerned. One conclusion we arrived at was that there had been a high degree of path dependency in the way policies towards hospitals and the police had been made and re-made over the period studied – in both countries. This path dependency appeared to be closely connected to the very different political systems of the two countries, which set the policymaking processes in radically different contexts, both structurally and in terms of process. Belgium had an increasingly decentralized, federal political system, with a number of political parties which often worked in coalitions. One also had strong connections between local politics and national politics, and a legalistic administrative culture. In the UK one had a very centralized, single party government, only weak connections between local politics and central government and a highly managerial approach to policy implementation. These overall institutional differences survived with only modest changes throughout the 40 years and heavily influenced policymaking and policy implementation, centrally and locally. Within this frame, however, a number of common factors could be identified which affected both Belgium and the UK, and both hospitals and the police. These included fundamental changes in operating technologies, and the spread of managerialist ideas and techniques (even if these were applied much more intensively in the UK than in Belgium). So these instruments and ideas for change were to a certain extent common to the two countries, but they were filtered into practice at different speeds and to different degrees by the contrasting frameworks of national and local institutions. Some "punctuations" could be identified in the Belgian and UK stories, but other forms of more gradual, long-term change were also apparent.

Another example of historical institutionalism was a study by Sundström (2006) of the development of management-by-results systems in the Swedish government from the 1960s onwards. Sundström made an intensive analysis of official documents over a 40-year period and conducted 40 interviews with key participants. He concluded that this rationalistic management technique had not survived for so long because of its results. In fact a long series of official reports had revealed recurrent problems in implementation. Instead, he argued, management-by-results (under varying labels) had been promoted and sustained by a fairly small group of officials located (mainly) in those central agencies that were supposed to "own" this technique. The conclusion had a strongly institutionalist flavour and identified a type of path dependency, but at the same time wanted to distinguish itself from the original March and Olsen logic of appropriateness:

> The study shows that this public management policy reform ... hasn't primarily been a story about rational adaptations to worldwide changes in economy or technology, or imitation due to government's disposition to follow rules and act appropriately. The course of events is better understood by forces of inertia inherent within Swedish public administration and the

way the PMP [Public Management Policy] sector has been organized and
regulated. (Sundström, 2006, p. 421)

2.6 Some big name theories: 2. rational choice and principal-agent theory

Rational choice theories begin with individuals rather than institutions. Their prime focus is on how individuals make choices. These
theories are leading examples of what in the social sciences is termed
"methodological individualism". That does not mean (as is inaccurately
claimed by some critics) that they ignore organizational or institutional factors. But it does mean that the individual is the active heart
of the theory, and institutions are important mainly in so far as they
provide a framework of incentives, penalties and rules within which
individuals make their calculations. Fundamentally, rational choice is
very different from neo-institutionalism.

In rational choice theory the individual actors make choices which they
believe will maximize their utility/best satisfy their preferences. In this
sense they act rationally. This rationality is often modelled in formal,
mathematical terms, and can yield quite precise predictions. Once the
researcher has specified the actor's preference schedule, hypotheses
can be generated and tested about how that actor will react to different
types of incentive and penalty. Actors are thus seen as instrumental
and calculative: they take those decisions which are best calculated to
satisfy their individual preferences. This is not the world of March and
Olsen's "logic of appropriateness".

Maximizing utility/satisfying preferences may sound like a beauti-
fully simple proposition but it is actually very complicated. It includes
within itself a number of puzzles. The main ones are listed below.

- What is utility? Some have accused rational choice theorists of
  using a model of wo/man which is totally selfish and self-seeking,
  and therefore unrealistic. However, while some applications
  of the theory can be like that, it is not an essential part of the
  theory. "Utility" and the related "preferences" are very general and
  flexible concepts. They could mean just making money. Or they
  could mean altruistically helping others: it all depends on what
  gives you satisfaction. Overall, however, it would probably be
  fair to say that most applications of rational choice theory do not

leave a lot of room for "other-regarding" actions (altruism, self-sacrifice, loyalty and so on). They assume that maximizing utility will be a "self-regarding" affair, that the dominant preferences will concern defending or increasing one's own income, power, enjoyment, status or freedom.

- Where do the actor's preferences come from? In much rational choice work preferences are treated as "endogenous". They are just there – given at the start of the analysis. This is, again, unlike neo-institutionalism where preferences are shaped and reshaped by upbringing, education and institutional cultures. However, in some more advanced applications of rational choice there is some analysis of preference formation. A well-known example is Dunleavy (2013) where the author theorizes how political parties do not merely try to please voters (that is, satisfy their existing – given – preferences) but more actively attempt to shape these preferences.

- How stable are these preferences? The more stable an actor's preferences are, the better rational choice theories work. If preferences are changing every minute, or are internally inconsistent, then it is hard to use the model of the utility-maximizing actor to make predictions. Most research that uses rational choice theory assumes that preferences are both stable and consistent/unconflicting. Yet this assumption is in conflict with a good deal of socio-psychological evidence about how individuals actually make decisions. The latter indicates that preferences often shift depending on circumstances and the way in which issues are framed (Hammond, 1996; Kahneman, 2012; March, 1994). The founding fathers of neo-institutionalist theory put this criticism forcefully: "Most research on preferences . . . indicates that preferences and meanings develop in politics, as in the rest of life, through a combination of education, indoctrination and experience. They are neither stable, nor precise, nor exogenous" (March and Olsen, 1989, p. 163).

- How accurate are the actor's perceptions of the course of action that will maximize their utility? Another way of putting this question would be to ask how well the actor makes use of the information potentially available to them. In a perfect world all the relevant information for a decision would be available, the actor would pay attention to all of it, and would then apply the correct logic to processing that information, so as to be able to choose the course of action that would maximize his or her preference satisfaction. Sometimes rational choice theorists are accused of – unrealistically – assuming perfect rationality. This criticism may have force in some cases, but it is not an accurate criticism of rational choice theories as a whole. In fact, many of them assume either limited information and/or bounded rationality – which happen to be much closer to what the psychologists and sociologists of decision-making tend to find when they investigate actual decision behaviour (Hammond, 1996; Kahneman, 2012; March, 1994).

- How can rational choice theories be tested empirically? The most common application of rational choice theory in PM is probably one where the hypotheses are formally stated, then a body of relevant quantitative data is subject to statistical analysis, after which the findings are examined to see if they show statistically significant correlations. The two most common limitations to this approach are (a) no direct evidence of preferences and (b) little or no consideration of other possible explanations/causes. The preferences criticism is a particularly significant one. The majority of rational choice papers in PM seem to assume what the actors' preferences will be rather than directly to investigate them. They are also assumed to be stable and logically coherent (see previous bullet point). If any direct evidence is sought it is usually via surveys. One has to ask, however, how reliable survey evidence is likely to be if one is asking politicians and/or officials about their innermost, most politically sensitive motivations.

Rational choice theory comes in different "flavours" (Peters, 2000, pp. 43–62). In one version institutions are conceived as sets of rules. Members of organizations or institutions accept the rules in exchange for membership benefits (pay, status security and so on). In a variant of this, institutions are collections of rules but the key rules are decision rules. "From the perspective of rationality, institutions provide a stable means of making choices in what would otherwise be an extremely contentious political environment" (Peters, 2000, p. 49). This kind of thinking encourages ideas of institutional design as an analysis which yields the optimum set of rules for an organization's purposes.

Another version – widely used in the study of regulatory and executive agencies – is called principal-agent theory (Douma and Schreuder, 1998). Here the central issue is the relationship between the principal (minister/boss/owner) and his or her agents (civil servants, employees, managers). How can the principal structure the relationship so that the agents (who naturally have preferences of their own) will have sufficiently powerful incentives to follow the preferences of the principal rather than their own? And how can the principal protect him or herself against the fact that the agents will often know more about the details of the business than the principal does him or herself ("information asymmetery")? How can the principal ensure compliance with his or her own wishes? Principal-agent theory seems to have its chief strength in the analysis of particular, dyadic relationships. It becomes progressively more difficult to apply (and to understand) when the situation is one where a public manager has multiple principals (for example, is accountable to her permanent secretary or chief executive, the national audit office, her professional association and to partner organizations involved in the joint delivery of services). Unfortunately, the existence of multiple principals (and agents) is rather common in today's public sector.

Game theory can also be thought of as a variety of rational choice. Here rational actors seek to satisfy their own preferences, but in a dynamic context where they are aware of the differing preferences of other actors, and attempt to adjust to them in an effort to get the best deal out of a given situation. Compliance is again a central issue in this type of theorizing – how can an actor be confident that another actor will honour their commitments? Game theory originated in mathematics, and some of the analyses involve advanced quantitative techniques. Game theorists try to model all the "moves" a set of self-interested actors might choose to make when they calculate what the other actors are likely to do, and to see whether there is a stable "solution" to a bargaining game, or not.

Yet another type of rational choice is described by Peters (2000, pp. 49–50) as "individuals within organizations". This is the one that probably comes closest (though that is not very close) to the neo-institutionalism we looked at in the previous section. It addresses organizations directly, but from the point of view of the utility-maximizing individual who is trying to use the organization instrumentally to satisfy his or her preferences. It is from this brand of rational choice that the once-influential idea has come that top bureaucrats, unless closely monitored, will always seek to expand their organizational budget and/or size. This notion of "empire-building" bureaucrats became very popular politically despite the lack of evidence to support it (and despite the fact that top bureaucrats in Europe and North America are currently dutifully carrying out major budget cuts).

Rational choice theories have aroused strong feelings among supporters and critics alike. One unfortunate consequence of this is that abstract arguments about these theories tend to degenerate into the positions of "all-for" or "all-against". Yet often there is nothing to prevent the combination of elements of these theories with other theories of different types. Indeed, some such combinations have proven rather fruitful. Take, for example, an investigation of delegation to independent regulatory agencies (IRAs) in four western European states (Thatcher, 2002). The author begins by taking the principal-agent hypothesis that delegation performs valuable functions for the delegating principal (in this case usually a politician). In particular, they enable those principals to make "credible committments", and, if the legislation forming the IRA is drawn up correctly, to reduce "shirking" (diverging preferences by the agent) and "slippage" (decisions made by agents which are not those that would have been made by the principals). Thatcher then goes on to look at the creation of agencies during the 1980s and 1990s in France, Germany, Italy and the UK. After careful analysis he comes to the following conclusion:

> Principal-agent frameworks offer an excellent starting point to analyse the delegation to IRAs. They point to the functional reasons that lead elected officials to choose to delegate, such as desires to shift blame, the need for credible committments and to respond to greater technical and international demands on national policymakers. In western Europe, delegation to IRAs aided elected officials to face new or increased pressures, such as those arising from privatisation, liberalisation, technological and economic developments, clashes between public opinion and desirable objectives, and the effects of supranational organisations. (Thatcher, 2002, pp. 142–3)

Yet while principal-agent theory offers a "good starting point" Thatcher readily concedes that:

> . . . a purely functionalist and formal institutional account of delegation is inadequate. (Thatcher, 2002, p. 143)

This is because the move to IRAs differed in speed, degree and extent between the different countries – and not necessarily in the ways which principal-agent theory might predict. So Thatcher invokes different framing conditions to enhance his explanation. He refers to political leadership, mimetic policy learning, and state traditions and structures. In other words he sets his principal-agent analysis within some neo-institutionalist scaffolding.

To conclude, I will very briefly describe two further applications of rational choice theories. The first was a comparative study of the creation of managerially autonomous tax collection agencies in various states in Africa and Latin America (Taliercio, 2004). Taliercio wanted to test a typical rational choice hypothesis: that taxpayers would be more likely to pay their taxes if they knew they were paying to a competent, autonomous tax collection agency than if they were paying to an inefficient ministry that was plagued with patronage and corruption. In theoretical terminology this was again another case of "credible commitment". Politicians by giving tax functions the status of an autonomous, professional agency could convince more taxpayers that revenue collection would not suffer political interference. Taliercio was able to make this test because in a number of countries (Kenya, South Africa, Uganda, Mexico, Venezuela and Peru) PM reforms had created more or less autonomous tax agencies. Using data from a survey, as well as a variety of other sources, he was able to show that autonomous tax collection agencies seemed to perform better than those existing before autonomization. Further, it looked as though the most autonomous agencies had made the biggest improvements in performance. In his conclusions, however, Taliercio made two important additional points. First, autonomy was not the only factor at work. It was not much good having more autonomy if an agency did not have the kind of professionally skilled managers who could make use of that autonomy. Second, he acknowledged that the reforms could be – and in some cases had been – undermined by political pressures from minsters and ministries which felt they had lost control (including control of a source of patronage and revenue) and wanted to regain it.

The second example is of a much broader and more ambitious treatment. Dunleavy's *Democracy, Bureaucracy and Public Choice* (1991 [2013]) showed what economic approaches to political science could achieve in the hands of a leading political scientist. Dunleavy elaborated the model of public choice so as to include both how political parties sought to shape voters' preferences (so no assumption that voters' preferences were just "given") and how senior officials pursued public management reforms that would make their own jobs easier and more rewarding. This second element ("bureau-shaping") is of particular relevance for PM. Dunleavy was critical of earlier rational choice models which posited that top bureaucrats would routinely aim to maximize the budgets of their bureau. His model of top bureaucrats' preferences was more subtle. Instead of just aiming for big budgets,

Dunleavy saw top officials as seeking the kinds of reform that would give them policy work rather than operational work, and which would give policy units higher status than operational units, and a high degree of control over the latter. Operational work is both boring (routine) and sometimes dangerous for reputations (a myriad of things can go wrong with complex public services, and on the front line operational managers often have to deal with difficult staff and demanding service users). However, being in policy or strategy units, located close to ministers, puts one at a distance from all these daily troubles, and what is more it offers interesting intellectual tasks critiquing and thinking up new policies. Therefore, Dunleavy argued, top officials would indulge in "bureau-shaping" – creating and promoting the kinds of reform that hived off operational tasks to executive agencies but left the top officials in small, high-powered analysis units close to the centres of power. The book also covered several other key issues in policymaking, but there is no room to summarize those here. *Democracy, Bureaucracy and Public Choice* is of additional interest because whereas rational choice theorists are sometimes accused of being politically right-wing neo-liberals, Dunleavy deliberately sets out to show that this body of theory can be used in a different way, sometimes in support of ideas more associated with the left than the right.

2.7   Some big name theories: 3. governance theories

Governance theories are more recent than both neo-institutionalism and rational choice. They have neither the individual actor nor the individual organization at their core. Rather they are focused on the entire system of governments, public agencies, firms, non-profit organizations, citizens' groups and popular "movements" which participate in public sector decision-making and in public service delivery. It is held that society has become more diverse, fragmented and complex, and therefore so has policymaking. If they want to formulate effective policies, governments are obliged to persuade and work with a wide range of non-governmental actors. Furthermore the delivery of policies also often involves other actors – contracted service companies, charities, non-profits and co-producing citizens (Alford and O'Flynn, 2012). This gives rise to close connections between the concept of governance and the concepts of networks and partnerships. In governance networks the different actors are interdependent – on most issues no one actor (even the government) has the authority or resources to command the others to do its bidding. So such networks are self-organizing, and function through trust and diplomacy rather than through command and control.

Different governance writers have started in different places and asked different kinds of questions about these ideas. Some political scientists have focused on explaining why (in their view) governance has replaced government – where has governance "come from"? One of the founding fathers of governance studies has argued that the waves of privatizations and contracting out that were carried out in some countries from the mid 1980s onwards indirectly and unintentionally contributed to the growth of governance (Rhodes, 2007). These market-oriented reforms fragmented the previous hierachical organizational forms, distanced much public service provision from direct government control and therefore created a need for coordination between relatively autonomous organizations.

Others have put forward a larger argument about the changing nature of society. They suggest that as society has become more complex (not simply fragmented, but better educated, richer and more "connected" through the digital media) the nature of the problems faced by governments has changed. Now governments increasingly have to deal with "wicked problems", where the nature of the problem as well as the possible solutions are deeply contested, and no one best scientifically legitimated answer can be agreed. The different interest groups ("stakeholders") are better organized and informed than ever before. And as the problems have become more difficult, so have the powers available to central (national) governments declined. Many of the wicked problems are international and can only be tackled through international cooperation (banking regulation, climate change, migration, trade agreements). Domestically, national governments no longer have the direct hierarchical "reach" they used to possess, because many formerly public functions have been privatized or contracted out. Further, in many countries, regional and local governments have pushed and continue to push for greater autonomy, so that governing becomes more and more a multi-level, multi-actor process. Frederickson, although highly critical of much of the relevant academic literature, concluded that "Governance, even with its weakness, is the most useful available concept for describing and explaining these forces" (2005, p. 292).

Other commentators have been more interested in the effects of governance, and how it can be the source of improved policymaking and implementation. Thus PM scholars have asked what types of governance networks there are, which types seem to be most effective and how they can be steered or managed (Koppenjan and Klijn, 2004). This literature has generated a whole range of roles and models of network processes – the need for "network managers", the new importance of "boundary spanning" roles, the usefulness of different kinds of process rules within networks, the strategies for connecting network actors and building trust between them and so on.

Governance theories have become very fashionable, and the academic literature has grown to enormous proportions. Practitioners have also picked up on at least some aspects of governance ideas – witness the international wave of government enthusiasm for partnerships, and the widespread discussions, in governments as well as academia, about "wicked problems" (for example, Ministry of Finance, 2013).

One major criticism of the governance school is that the concept itself is unstable, and has been the subject of a kind of taxonomic frenzy (Frederickson, 2005, pp. 285–6; Pollitt and Hupe, 2011). A standard academic text opened with two experts offering, respectively, five and seven different meanings for governance (see Hirst, 2000; Rhodes, 2000). Kooiman (1999) came to a classification of ten different ways in which the term "governance" has appeared in the literature. Other labels are "new governance" and "multiple governance". Beyond that we have "co-governance", "institutional co-governance", "collaborative governance", "governance networks", "hybrid governance", "operational governance" and "meta-governance". An overview (Osborne, 2010, pp. 6–7) broadly accepts this diversity. He distinguishes "public governance" from "corporate governance" and "good governance" and then goes on to classify five sub-types. No wonder Bovaird and Löffler (2003, p. 316) considered defining governance as like trying to "nail a pudding on the wall".

Another problem is the patchy nature of empirical evidence. Many scholars affirm that networks have grown more common, more powerful and more necessary – but where is the evidence (Pollitt, 2003, pp. 52–74)? Few publications actually count networks, and even fewer attempt directly to measure their power or influence. Similarly, governments themselves are supposed to be weaker – indeed, "hollowed out" according to some leading governance theorists. But again, where is the systematic evidence for this claim? The preponderance of governance literature is concerned with particular case studies and does not (and cannot) address these wider questions of representativeness. It is not clear how far "governance" is principally a metaphor, a method, an analytical scheme or a theory.

A core concern is the "woolliness" of much of the governance theorizing. Large, abstract concepts are plentiful, testable hypotheses are few. Like some varieties of neo-institutionalism – and rational choice – some governance analyses would appear to be unfalsifiable. Some of the more abstract material appears to have become almost context-free: "new public governance" is discussed at length with very little anchoring to the specifics of different countries' different political systems, cultures, legal systems and so on (Osborne, 2010). Yet the probability of finding "one best way" of steering networks that could be applied in all the myriad of circumstances in which public policies are implemented, in Sweden and Swaziland, must be vanishingly small.

Finally, there are normative concerns. If public policies are to be made and delivered through complex, self-regulating networks of inter-dependent organizations, how can the classic principles of public accountability be applied? How can continuity and security of service be assured? And how can these systems be designed to prevent the quiet takeover of public functions by corporate interests – the term "partnership" sounds close and trustful, but there is evidence that big corporations are sometimes able to use "partnering" to establish very extensive influence over sectors of government policy and practice (Wilks, 2013). Last but not least, how effective is network governance at solving the kinds of problems that allegedly led to its emergence? There have been studies of network effectiveness, but it is a difficult area and many of the measures that have been used have been essentially measures of process (were all stakeholders included in the decision-making?) rather than measures of outcomes (did the health/education/water supply of the community actually improve?).

2.8   Small theories

The big name theories are far from being the only type of theory in play in PM. Many theories operate and at a much more detailed level and have narrower, more particularistic applications.

One example can be taken from J.Q. Wilson's classic *Bureaucracy* (1989). Wilson analysed the functions of public agencies and came to the conclusion that different agencies performed fundamentally

Table 2.1 J.Q. Wilson's typology of public agencies (1989)

Outputs observable?	Outcomes observable?	
	Yes	No
Yes	A. Production organizations	B. Procedural organizations
No	C. Craft organizations	D. Coping organizations

Note: Examples of Production organizations = driving licence agency, Procedural organizations = mental health counselling, Craft organizations = forest rangers, Coping organizations = diplomatic service. An organization may well have several functions and these may be located in different cells. Changes in technology may shift a function from one cell to another by making aspects of it more observable than in the past.

different types of task, and that these task differences demanded different approaches to management. A mental health counselling service could not be managed (or not successfully) using the same approach as the management of, say, an agency that issued driving licences.

Wilson argued that two crucial features were whether the outcomes of the agency's actions could be directly observed and whether the outputs of the agency's actions could be directly observed. Here outcomes mean the final results out there in the world, while outputs mean what the organization directly produces or delivers. Thus, for example, an environmental health inspectorate would produce various reports and data on air and water quality (outputs) but however good these were it would not necessarily mean that the actual quality of the air and the water (outcomes) got better. Wilson reasoned that if both the outputs and the outcomes could be observed (in his terms a "production" organization) then there was the basis for a fairly tight, target-driven style of management. Top management could specify the desirable outcomes and also the outputs necessary to achieve those outcomes, and then the actual achievement of these outputs and outcomes could be closely monitored and the staff rewarded accordingly. At the other corner of the matrix, however, both the outputs and the outcomes of some public sector organizations were ambiguous or hidden from view (for Wilson, "coping organizations"). If management tried to run a coping organization mainly by specifying precise outputs and outcomes this was unlikely to work well. It would be better, in these circumstances, to set some very broad objectives, to try to build and maintain a particular culture of trust and commitment to public service, and then to give front line staff a measure of discretion as to how they operated. This is a very crude summary of the rather subtle set of inferences Wilson set out, but it should be apparent that this can be a very fruitful kind of mid-level theorizing.

Other small theories are smaller still. Take, for example, some of the ideas around the use of performance-related pay (PRP). At the core is the idea that staff will work harder or smarter, or both, if they know that their measured performance – if it is high-scoring – will bring them additional pay, or some kind of extra acknowledgement or privileges (for example, more training or free time). If the positive incentive is money (that is, a bonus) one crucial question is: "how much extra money is necessary to generate improved performance?" Obviously paying bonuses that are too small (say a $10 dollar bonus to an employee who is earning $50 000 basic pay) is pointless. On the other hand, paying huge bonuses is wasteful if the extra sum is more than would have been necessary to incentivize the staff to improve. So how much is enough? Some studies have led to the hypothesis that a bonus needs to represent at least 10 per cent of the individual's salary before it will have a direct incentive effect on their performance. Of course this needs to be tested in a variety of contexts (it may not be the same percentage for low and high paid staff; it may not be the same percentage in different work cultures) but having some theory as to where this threshold may be is clearly an important factor in the design of PRP schemes. A roughly similar problem arises around the question of what proportion of staff should receive bonuses. A very small percentage may mean that most staff cannot see that a bonus is worth aiming for anyway. A very large percentage receiving bonuses would remove any particular status attaching to an award – and would probably also be very expensive! Some of these "smaller" theoretical issues are refreshingly discussed in Perry et al. (2009).

2.9 Theories with no name

Many pages are written about the big theories but at the same time a lot of theory creeps into PM scholarship without ever being given a name. Sometimes this happens because the author(s) does not want to be identified with a particular theoretical school of thought, but sometimes it may occur unconsciously. For example, the author just wants to explain phenomenon X or Y, and produces a particular form of explanation, based on the evidence, without ever thinking "I am going to use/have been using theory A or theory B". So theories without any particular label are quite common in academic PM. There is no reason to consider them as in any general way inferior to big name theories or other, "branded" theoretical products.

One quick example of this would be an article in a leading PM journal concerning the use of discretion by "street level" operational staff (Tummers and Bekkers, 2014). These authors investigated the idea that a measure of discretion for front line service deliverers would strengthen the implementation of policies in two ways. First, the ability of staff to use discretion to tailor the service (within limits) to the particular needs of the individual client would be meaningful to that client. Second, the sense of having some discretion and not being just automata, tied to a very detailed rulebook, would enhance the willingness of the staff to implement the policy. Furthermore, there was an interaction between these two effects. Because doing something for clients was an important part of the rationale for service delivery staff, the realization that discretion was appreciated by those clients would further reinforce staff willingness to implement the policy. Tummers and Beckkers took a survey of 1317 Dutch mental healthcare professionals and applied factor analysis and a structural equation model to the responses to questions concerned with discretion. They found the ideas described above confirmed by this statistical analysis. They also identified some limitations to their research design (for example, clients had not been directly questioned, only service providers) and suggested further research that could extend our understanding of discretion. But nowhere in this useful piece of research did the authors fly the flag of some named theory – they simply set out their propositions, tested them and discussed the results.

2.10   Post-modernism in PM

Post-modernism is hard to classify. Its scope is enormous, but its achievements in applications to the mainstream themes of academic PM is much more limited (partly, no doubt, because post-modernists regard some of the traditional preoccupations of the field as pointless and unachievable). So I have positioned it here in its own section. Its following among PM scholars could not be described as particularly extensive, and its publications seldom feature in the leading mainstream PM journals. Nevertheless, it has its own band of followers, its own journals and conferences and its own heroes and villains.

Post-modern scholars have made a major contribution in deconstruct-ing the surfaces of texts and analysing political and bureaucratic rheto-ric and storytelling. They have assembled a powerful critique of modern technocratic rationalism (Bogason, 2005), though they are not the only ones to have done this. But what is post-modernist theory? That is hard to say, because the term itself is not much used by "pomos". Certainly it is not a general theory (generalizations are usually regarded with suspicion and criticism) and it does not claim to be objective (the very notion of objectivity is rejected). Furthermore the post-modernist camp is itself riven with distinctions and disagreements.

Both the ontology and epistemology of post-modernism are different from the theories we have looked at thus far. Many pomos have strong doubts about whether "external reality" is accessible to us at all and, even if it is, that is not the focus of their work. Epistemologically they are deeply critical of the whole paraphernalia of methods deployed by "modernist" or "empiricist" social scientists. Instead they emphasize words – texts – and the interpretations of those texts. But they are not looking for the "correct" interpretation. Typically they play with a range of interpretations, sometimes claiming that *all* interpretations have equal status and claim upon our attention. Some of the strongest work in the pomo portfolio is aimed at "deconstructing" widely used arguments and terminology from mainstream PM. Thus, for example, a pomo scholar might point out that while there are acres of main-stream discussion about how to define and achieve "efficiency", the term itself actually has multiple meanings within different groups and cultures, and in some does not exist at all (Bogason, 2005, p. 241). Thus there is no "objective", externally existing thing called efficiency; rather it is a concept developed by particular groups in particular times and places for particular purposes. And those purposes are overwhelmingly those of modernist, rational organizations which are concerned with control and productivity. Thus "efficiency" is part of a particular kind of rhetoric and can be interpreted as such.

Among some pomo PM scholars – particularly the American ones – there has also been a tendency to emphasize the advantages of citizen participation, citizen experience and localism. All these things come from or facilitate the voicing of a variety of everyday experiences. The latter are seen as potentially more powerful and authentic than the dry analyses of modernist "science" (Bogason, 2005, pp. 248–9). Technocratic solutions are rejected because the claims to better knowledge made by the technocratic elite are seen as false.

It is very difficult to summarize these various strands. Perhaps a flavour can be given by the following brief citation from a leading American post-modernist PM scholar:

> Theory is to be used instrumentally for changing unsatisfactory conditions in the world, and subjective understandings of such conditions matter to the scholar in such work. Qualitative not quantitative measures are important, and it is not possible to elevate any reasoning above other reasonings because of the application of a particular method. Instrumental use of theory must be justified by the conditions of the case, one cannot use generalized theory to classify action. Scholars have the same right as anyone else to be normative. (Farmer, 1995, p. 72)

Despite the refreshing and occasionally entertaining character of pomo PM, the more radical claims of some post-modern PM scholars can be regarded as destructive of the basic rationale for the whole field (yes, this is one of the moments where you are hearing my personal opinion!). A PM which is reduced solely to the interpretation of texts and stories, which denies or doubts the existence of an external reality, which attacks any notion of causation, and which holds all interpretations to be in some sense equally valid, is no longer PM as most of us know it. (Each of these claims has been made somewhere in the post-modernist corpus of academic publications.)

Here are two typical statements by well-known authors in PM and public policy who are taking up post-modern positions:

> A fact is a piece of evidence that nearly everyone in a given community would accept as true . . . We define objectivity as evaluation by comparing rival stories. (Bevir and Rhodes, 2006, p. 28)

and

> Phenomena can only be understood within the context in which they are studied; findings from one context cannot be generalized to another. (Guba and Lincoln, 1989, p. 45)

The first of these statements carries the implication that everything one might wish or need to study in PM is best conceived of as a narrative. It further suggests that the central activity for PM academics is comparing rival accounts. While comparing rival accounts may well be an activity many academics will need to undertake, the suggestion that this is the main or even only task for public policy and PM academics amounts to an enormous restriction. One can also think of many uncomfortable implications that would flow from acceptance of this dictum. If a given community strongly held racist or sexist views, would that make them "facts"? The second statement is even more limiting. It implies that the whole mission of traditional social science is unworkable. No generalizations that "travel" are possible, it claims. If so, one can see no reason why the public should pay much attention to academics, or, indeed, why the taxpayers should be prepared to fund them. They become local storytellers, with no wider contribution to offer.

However, a few post-modernists have made valiant efforts to suggest that their approach *is* capable of conducting empirical, socially relevant research. Some try to redefine what it might mean – very cautiously – to generalize (Bogason, 2005, p. 246). These attempts remain unconvincing (my opinion, again). Alvesson (2002) is one example of a leading scholar who has tried to make "pomo" fit for empirical social research. In his book he is driven to seperate "hard core pomo" from moderate pomo, and then tries to build bridges between the moderates and other post-positivist approaches. Even then, the kind of empirical research that can be envisaged is painfully narrow. The idea that no form of reasoning can be elevated above any other form of reasoning (Bogason, 2005, p. 252) would appear to put the whole edifice of policy analysis and evaluation – not to speak of the reasoned choice of public policies by elected representatives – on thin ice. In fact, of course, most post-modernists clearly *do* put some forms of reasoning above others – their whole critique of rationalistic modernism is based on the belief that a qualitative, interpretive, contextualized approach is superior. They are foes of generalization, except for the huge generalization that generalizations are inadmissable. They are resistant, if not hostile, to those post-positivist realists who struggle to construct context-sensitive middle level generalizations (for example, Pawson, 2013).

Post-modernism has little to say to those many PM academics – and practitioners – who still believe that they *can* engage with an external reality and that some ways of doing so are – in certain types of context – likely to be more successful than others. This may be why an element of mainstream exasperation creeps in on those rare occasions when "empiricists" and post-moderns actually get into structured dialogue (Andrews et al., 2008; Luton, 2008; Lynn et al., 2008).

2.11   Time, change, stability and public management

Decisions, activities and organizations – the heartlands of PM – all exist in time (Pollitt, 2008). They are each, if you like, temporal processes. True, some decisions may be taken on the spur of the moment (and some have to be, as in the emergency services) but one would hope most big government decisions would be the product of mature reflection, the examination of evidence over a period of time,and the discussion of different options with a range of stakeholders. Activities also take time – one cannot build a motorway or airfield or hospital, or train a doctor, or negotiate an international trade agreement in days or even months. And organizations, as both rational choicers and neo-institutionalists recognize in their different ways, exist to provide a certain order and predictability over time. We know, from many studies, that while one may be able to alter the formal structures of organizations quite quickly, shifting the culture is quite a different matter.

It is therefore surprising that some of our practices in academic PM seem to take little account of the temporal dimension. Writing of American PA one scholar summarized that:

> The study of public administration pays little attention to history. Most publications are focused on current problems (the present) and desired solutions (the future) . . . This view of history is the product of a diminished and anemic sense of time, resulting from organizing the past as a series of events that inexorably lead to up to the present in a linear fashion . . . public administration scholarship needs to reacquaint itself with the nature of time. (Raadschelders, 2010, p. 235)

Many studies have the character of snapshots – a survey here, a cross-sectional statistical correlation there, the critical analysis of the latest reform. These can certainly be useful, but by themselves they can seldom be adequate to investigate how things may develop over time. There may be longer-term cycles or tendencies which are not picked up by cross-sectional (synchronic) research. To identify such patterns one needs some kind of temporal dimension in one's theories – and methods. There are many possibilities here, ranging from narrative histories to complex statistical time series, and each of these can reveal new facets and may suggest new kinds of explanation (Pollitt, 2008). The "big theories" we looked at earlier each contain some awareness of the temporal dimension (but that does not necessarily mean that this translates into a sophisticated treatment of time). In game theory (rational choice), for example, it is important to know whether a given game will be played only once, or will be repeated. If the former, the optimal strategies for the players are likely to be different than if the game is repetitive. A referendum on a particular issue, for example, may be a one-off event, whereas a budget is usually an annual process. In neo-institutionalism, as we have seen, there has been an extended discussion about path dependency.

Paying attention to time entails looking at the past as well as trying to estimate how long things will take, or what directions they will head in, in the future. Yet much PM scholarship seems to have shortened its attention span – to be focused mainly on current initiatives and short-term future options and innovations. That strikes me as unfortunate. In an earlier work, I summed up the matter thus:

> [W]hile we can try to ignore the past, it will not let us alone. In concrete terms, the majority of laws, policies, people and buildings will continue to come from the past, often from the quite distant past. They will have been formed and influenced by past circumstances and, while these earlier influences can often be overlain or supressed, they can seldom be entirely eliminated. It is extremely difficult to avoid time's arrows, or to suddenly jump off its cycles. The past inevitably constrains the present in a myriad of ways, and more positively, it also shapes future opportunities. One of these ways is by influencing our time perspectives themselves, including our knowledge of the varying fates of previous innovations and our understanding of the time perspectives and time tactics of the others with whom we work and live. (Pollitt, 2008, p. 184)

2.12 Contexts

PM scholars frequently refer to contextual factors. For example, current public management reforms in Europe and North America are often said to be undertaken in the context of fiscal austerity, or we are told that the weakness and fading of certain reforms in central and eastern European countries needs to be seen in the context of the post-Communist heritage of low-skilled, poorly paid public services. There is a widespread, though far from universal, recognition of the need to put issues in context.

What, however, is the relationship of context to theory? That is often left unclear. Too often theory and context are treated as quite seperate. The theory is regarded as the active part and the context is like the scenery in a traditional theatre – a static, passive back-drop against which the action takes place. Also, "context" may be used to hoover up any bits and pieces which the theory does not seem to deal with – in this role contexts become a kind of trash bin for untidy left-overs. Elsewhere I have argued that these are unsatisfactory approaches to context (Pollitt, 2013a). Context itself needs to be theorized (and before that defined in reasonably specific terms). It can be factual (the finance ministry had ordered 20 per cent budget cuts) or conceptual (the climate surrounding the reform was one in which neo-liberal ideas of public sector inefficiency and the efficiency-driving properties of market competition were dominant). Context is also usually multiple – the climate of thought may be one dimension for a specific reform or decision, but at the same time there may be relevant technological change taking place and/or shifts in the framework of professional regulation or the emergence of a new pattern of political parties (Pollitt, 2013b). Further, contexts are better conceived of as constitutive of action rather than purely passive and static. For example, when a newly appointed hospital chief executive decides that the hospital needs a new strategic plan, and sets that action in train, she may have been influenced by both (a) a climate of thought which includes the idea that strategic plans are a necessary symbol of modern organizational management and (b) an awareness that technological change means that many primary care centres can now perform medical procedures which were previously the exclusive preserve of hospitals. Therefore a strategic plan will serve both legitimation and functional needs. This idea of contexts as active constituents leads to a need to examine the mechanisms and processes that enable contexts to have constitutive effects (these will often be processes leading to the formation of dominant views of certain situations, and will involve professional networks, politicized media and so on). Finally, contexts often play a particularly important role in international comparisons. If one compares the limited implementation of NPM ideas in the German federal government as compared with UK central government during the 1980s and 1990s, the differing contexts will probably play a major part in one's explanation (Pollitt and Bouckaert, 2011). The unshiftable constitution and the general dominance of legalistic thinking in Germany contrasted with a very plastic set of procedural requirements and a managerialist climate of thought in the UK. Furthermore, given that decentralization and autonomization were important components in NPM thought, it was a relevant contextual factor that Germany was already a highly decentralized country while the UK was, by European standards, unusually centralized and "top-heavy". So they started from very different places.

In short, contexts are often important, and need to be integrated with the main theoretical approaches being used, not just tacked on as an afterthought.

2.13   Personal footnote

I will permit myself a concluding footnote. It is to observe that, on the whole, I would rather read a good scholar wrestling to apply a weak theory than a mediocre scholar working with a strong theory. I mention this here because in my experience (and I know from many conversations with colleagues that the experience is not mine alone) *applying* theory is one of the skills that students have the greatest difficulty with. Many are perfectly competent with theory and equally good at conducting empirical research but simply cannot bring the two into active, detailed connection with each other. This may be partly because these two dimensions of the subject – theory and methods – are often taught seperately. At any event, the application of theories to empirical material is something which requires practice, practice and then more practice. It comes to few of us naturally. Apart from practice, the other experience that can help is to see examples of scholars working hard in the way I have described. Among those I would recommend are Hood (1998) (cultural theory applied to "the art of the state"), March (1994) (reviewing a range of theories about how we make decisions) and Pawson (2013) (a vigorous sorting-through of various theories of evaluation). Last but not least, there is the revised version of an absolute classic: Allison and Zelikow's *Essence of Decision: Explaining the Cuban Missile Crisis* (1999) in which the authors carefully contrast and compare three alternative theoretical approaches to the same evidence base.

2.14   Key reading

There is no obvious single book – no "bible" – that can tell PM scholars all they need or might wish to know about theory. However, there are some excellent expositions of major theoretical "schools" and issues. None of them are comprehensive but they do cover a lot of ground. These recommendations can be supplemented with the more detailed references on specific issues and cases given in the main body of the text (above).

One key text is Guy B. Peters's *Institutional Theory in Political Science: The New Institutionalism*. In this chapter I have referenced the original edition (2000), but you should look for the latest edition. One advantage of this book is that the author covers what rational choice theories have to say about institutions, as well as the more obvious brands of historical institutionalism and sociological institutionalism.

James March and Johan Olsen are frequently credited with having launched the "new institutionalism". An early book which is still well worth exploring is *Rediscovering Institutions: The Organizational Basis of Politics* (1989).

Finally, I refer again to a book I mentioned in the previous section – Ray Pawson's *The Science of Evaluation: A Realist Manifesto* (2013). Evaluating public sector programmes and projects is a core task for many PM scholars, and for practitioners too. The evaluation "industry" has grown and diversified since the 1970s. In this work Pawson shows just how hard – but rewarding – it is to follow through from broad philosophical underpinnings to more specific theories to practical applications that generate reliable findings. It includes a good deal of discussion of methods as well as theory. Written in his characteristically amusing and combative style, it will repay close reading.

3   Methods and approaches

> Epistemology is concerned with the philosophy of how we can
> know, methodology is focused on the practice of how we can know.
> (Raadschelders, 2011, p. 5)

3.1   Introduction

Within the PM academic community arguments over methods are as
common as arguments over theories. These arguments are important
for several reasons, one major one being that it is often said that it is the
method that guarantees (or undermines) the quality of the information
gained. Thus, for example, if you are interested in problems of alcohol-
ism and you choose the method of asking a sample of people exactly
how much they drink each week the quantities you record will almost
certainly be an underestimate of the amounts actually consumed. This
is because it has been shown that many of us underestimate, or actively
conceal, the true extent of our drinking. So the method of simply
asking people is weak – not totally useless by any means, but not very
accurate either. Yet on other, less sensitive topics, asking people may
turn out to be a very sound and fruitful way forwards.

Many social science books which deal explicitly with methods never
actually define the term. And there is widespread use of parallel or
overlapping terms such as tools, instruments, techniques and methodologies. So academic usage is often confusing or inconsistent. This
is not surprising, since different ontological and epistemological positions lead social scientists to assign varying roles to methods, and,
indeed, to conceptualize them in different ways. One line through
this confusion is to say that methods are specific, formal tools for
collecting or analysing empirical data. This leaves methods as quite
narrow entities – technical procedures such as factor analysis or semi-
structured interviews. I have some sympathy for this position, but my
problem is that I want to discuss more than this. Since the aim here

is to take a broad look at what PM scholars *do* when they embark on research I have included certain steps or procedures which would lie outside the rather narrow line on methods just described. For example, I spend time discussing literature reviews, although it could be argued that they do not constitute a method as such. Neither is comparative research a method (although it uses many methods). It is, however, a very common and valuable approach or strategy for empirical research. Therefore, I have not tried to solve the terminological complexity around "methods", but have merely attempted to circumnavigate it by titling the chapter "Methods *and approaches*".

It is not feasible to give a full account of PM methods within the space of one chapter. There are at least two reasons for this. One is the huge range of methods which are being and have been used by scholars – everything from factor analysis to unstructured participant observation, from Boolean algebra to the analysis of corporate storytelling, and from experiments to the careful reading of historical documents. The other reason is perhaps less obvious. It is that there is a significant element of craft in the choice of methods. (This observation is the cousin of the one in the previous chapter about having to learn how to apply theory.) The best available methods will be determined by the precise research question(s) being asked, but also by the circumstances in which the research is going to be carried out. A method of data collection that may be adequate in a country with good administrative record-keeping, a culture favouring open government and a cadre of public servants who are used to dealing with academic researchers will fail when applied in a country with an authoritarian, secretive culture and a lack of sympathy for inquisitive outsiders. Other, more mundane issues may also enter into the equation. For example, some methods may simply demand more time than the researcher has available (I have lost count of the number of doctoral students who, when they emerge from the library stage to start their fieldwork, have been taken aback by how long it can take to set up a programme of interviews with senior officials).

Fortunately, however, there are a number of good book-length methods guides already available (and this corpus is constantly being added to). A few are specifically directed at PM students (Van Thiel, 2014) but many are broader, being offered for public policy and politics students or for social scientists generally (for example, Maggetti et al., 2013; Robson, 2002). These are, in the main, helpful works but, at the same time, you need to be aware that each has its own preferred set of approaches, even if the authors strive to remain fairly inclusive. Thus, for example, both Van Thiel (2014) and Maggetti et al. (2013), though broad-minded and flexible in many ways, are unsympathetic to radical constructivist or post-modernist treatments. That is understandable, at least to the extent that radical constructivist and post-modern approaches tend to say little about research methods per se or, indeed, actively downgrade the importance that more orthodox academic researchers give them. Within the "applied phronesis" school, for example, we find one chapter section headed, "The question is not 'which method'? but 'what matters?'" (Schram, 2012, p. 20). The priority, in this radical view, is to deal with interesting and important topics, and methodological considerations come a poor second. My own take on this is that this is not a choice we are obliged to make. I can see no reason why PM scholars should not (a) deal with what matters *and* (b) do so with the best means available. The most appropriate means will vary according to the subject matter and the type of question being asked, but for any given research problem, some methods will be better than others.

So what *can* this chapter offer? My aim will be to achieve the following:

1. To locate the discussion of methods and approaches within the wider frame of research design.
2. To offer a perspective on the much debated issue of whether to use quantitative or qualitative methods.
3. To give a broad idea of what the range of methods used by PM scholars are – and here I have perforce had to make a selection, just as I did with theories in Chapter 2.
4. To provide a brief introduction to some of the more frequently used methods and approaches. This will not (and cannot) be a training in exactly how to use them (for that you need to go to methods books such as those mentioned above) but it will attempt to sensitize you to the broad character, and principal strengths and weaknesses of these methods and approaches.
5. To offer some observations about practical issues such as access and time. These perhaps mundane, but often crucial, issues are neglected in some methods books but frequently loom large as unavoidables in real-world research. They are central to what was referred to above as the craft element in research.

This is a large canvas to cover, so this chapter is longer than the other chapters in the book.

3.2 Designing research

One useful way of thinking about methods and approaches is is to locate them within a broader notion of research design (Maggetti et al., 2013, pp. 9–13; Van Thiel, 2014, pp. 55–60). This helps one avoid some of the more sterile debates about which method is (in the abstract) best. It makes it clear that the optimal method or methods are the ones that fit best with the other key elements in the overall design. The "key elements" usually look something like this:

1. The chosen research question(s) or problem(s).
2. The chosen key concepts.
3. The chosen theory or theories.
4. The chosen methods.
5. The context in which the research will have to take place – including questions of available time, access, cost and skills available to the researcher(s).

While the research problem or question usually comes first, it would be a mistake to suppose that all these elements usually get settled in this strict order – concepts before theories, theories before methods and so on. Occasionally PM research may be as neat as this, but very often it is not. A more common experience is that a process of mutual adjustment takes place between items two to five on the above list (and from time to time even item one may need to be modified). This is why the word "chosen" is included in each of the first four items – because each of these needs to be actively, thoughtfully chosen, and sometimes that choice will need to be revisited after the research has got underway.

One of the most common failings in doctoral research – and sometimes even in major international PM research projects – is that the researchers become committed (and are sometimes obliged by funders to become committed) to a particular research question, theoretical approach and set of methods at an early stage. Later, they discover that the question is unanswerable in its original form, or that the key concepts adopted are too fuzzy, or that the methods are inappropriate for the question, or that key data are not available, or that in some other sense the "bits"of the design do not fit well together. But they cannot or will not make major changes, because the waggon is already rolling.

Consider how one might research the effects of fiscal austerity on the public sector in different countries. There would first be a need for considerable discussion about what did and did not constitute "austerity". Unless that could be settled reasonably clearly then the research could not go forward (the term austerity has been very widely used over the past few years but defining it in operational terms is quite difficult – see Hood et al., 2014). One would look, of course, at what scholars had already said about the impacts of austerity, and would discover a range of theories and hypotheses, some mainly concerned with economic aggregates like public expenditure and GDP growth, and others more focused on the effects on organizations (morale, service quantity and quality and so on). Some of these theories would directly contradict each other or, at least, would be based on widely varying assumptions (Blyth, 2013). Choices would need to be made about which of these existing ideas were most interesting and useful. Then, once all this was settled, one could investigate what kind of official data was available. This would probably show that different governments collected different data in somewhat different ways, and that from time to time they changed their own data systems, so that comparing figures over considerable periods of time posed considerable difficulties. For some hypotheses little or no reliable and relevant data might be available, especially if one was hoping to compare different countries or different periods. Much of the data about effects (for example, the effects of cuts on civil service morale or on service quality to the public) might be tantalising but hard to attribute with certainty to austerity, because of other trends going on at the same time (for example, changes to programme design, the ageing of the workforce, the introduction of new information technology (IT)). Other data could just be very hard to come by, either because public authorities wanted to conceal it or because they – deliberately or inadvertently – never collected it. This is often the case when outcomes have been unpopular – declining services, failures to meet targets, reforms that have never achieved their stated goals. Governments simply do not wish those kinds of stories to get around. So some of the original hypotheses might need to be set on one side as, temporarily at least, relatively untestable. Yet this can itself be useful in so far as it shows that some popular or taken-for-granted ideas actually lack any basis in evidence – for example, the idea that governments *never* cut spending unless faced with powerful external pressures, or the idea that harsh fiscal squeeze will *inevitably* lead to the governing parties losing the next election (Hood et al., 2014, p. 267). Equally, close inspection of the data that *is* available might well suggest some new questions or hypotheses that could be added to the research agenda. In short, a research design may well need to be adjusted as the research proceeds – it is, after all, *research*, that is, an investigation of as yet unknowns. The important thing is to have a design, so that new developments and discoveries can be seen in relation to the overall programme at any given time, even if that design occasionally has to be adjusted.

The example given above is of what one might term "big question research". Asking about the effects of austerity on different national public sectors is a big question covering many different dimensions, organizations and activities. For smaller questions it may be less difficult to come up with a design that will survive relatively unchanged throughout the period of research. An example would be a project I was involved in during the early 1990s in the UK (although I will take the discussion further than we were actually able to go). The situation was that central government had decided that "citizens' charters" were a good idea, and had instructed all local authorities to develop their own such charters. These charters were to incorporate brief statements of the rights of citizens with respect to local services (schools, refuse collection and so on) and would also set out the commitments of those managing the services (we will collect household waste at least once per week; we will see that all children in school have access to certain subjects and activities up to certain levels and so on). The research question was: "How far have local authorities implemented this policy?" In research terms this was much more manageable than: "What are the effects of fiscal austerity, internationally?"

The central pillar of the design was to ask local authorities what they had done. Given that there are roughly 180 such local governments in the UK one could either survey all of them or survey a sample. Either way, it was important to see that the surveys went to the right people in each authority (those who would know and could answer authoritatively) and that, if possible, some incentive was offered to encourage replies (a low response rate would render the research findings suspect). Typically, researchers would offer to feed back the findings to each authority (perhaps as a short policy brief) and to give free workshops for officers. Also, it might be helpful if the researchers could say that the national association of local authorities had approved their project.

If a sampling approach was taken it would be important to structure the sample so as to include representative numbers of large authorities and small authorities; urban authorities and rural authorities;

and authorities where the majority was held by each of the major political parties. This is because there are the beginnings of possible explanations nestling within these contrasting dimensions. Perhaps large authorities are better equipped to set up charters? Perhaps urban authorities are more dynamic and will implement the policy more vigorously? Perhaps, if the central government is Conservative, Conservative-dominated local authorities will implement the policy more enthusiastically than Labour-dominated local authorities?

All in all, then, with this type of project one could hope to make a clear research design at the beginning, and then stick to it. The result would be a set of findings which showed how far the policy had been implemented, and which drew attention to any patterns (larger authorities have gone further than smaller ones and so on). But this would only be the beginning. If patterns emerged the next question is obviously: "Why?" To answer that would probably require a different set of methods. Structured or semi-structured interviews of responsible staff in contrasting authorities would be one method. The aim would be to identify the processes that led to one type of authority implementing faster or further than another. Another extension of the original question would be to check to see if citizens were actually aware of these charters. What percentage of citizens had noticed that they existed? What percentage knew something about what was in them? Was there a pattern to this awareness (older citizens more knowledgable than younger ones; highly educated citizens more attentive than the less educated and so on)? Extending the original question in these ways would, therefore, require further research designs and a great deal of extra effort.

3.3   Quantitative versus qualitative?

In PM, as in many social science subjects, one encounters debates about whether quantitative or qualitative methods are best. I must confess to a certain irritation with such arguments which, when cast in these broad terms, I regard as largely pointless. There are several reasons why I take this impatient view.

First, it surely depends to a large extent on what research questions one is trying to respond to. For example, "How prevalent are members of ethnic minorities in the civil service?" is a question that demands at least a substantial component of counting. On the other hand, a research project on "How was the concept of public accountability articulated in France, Italy and the UK, 2000–15?" may contain some quantitative elements but will probably mainly require a qualitative description and comparison of language, concepts and cultures. In short, the optimal methods are those which fit best with the wider research design.

Second, there is often confusion around the term "quantitative". Many texts by "qualitative" social scientists may contain lots of numbers, tables and graphs – yet apparently that does not make them examples of "quantitative methods". Thus a history of the civil service may contain figures showing the numbers of civil servants and the trajectory of their salaries, but it would still be classified by many social scientists as a historical narrative – a traditional, qualitative treatment. The real dividing line, to such academics, is not the mere inclusion of numbers – of descriptive statistics. Rather it is the deployment of forms of inferential statistics or statistical analysis. It is the use of techniques such as regression analysis, variance analysis, significance tests, factor analysis and structural equation modelling, plus the construction of scales and weighted indices which mark out the territory of the "quants" (Van Thiel, 2014, pp. 128–37).

Third, the debate is still sometimes introduced as an either/or choice. Should you choose quantitative or qualitative methods? Yet this is often a false choice, in the sense that the strongest research design will very frequently combine both quantitative *and* qualitative methods. If you want to study why some public organizations seem regularly to innovate and others hardly ever seem to do so, should you use quantitative or qualitative methods? Answer: if possible, you should use both. You need to count the numbers of innovations as closely as you can (partly just to make sure that the initial impressions of different rates were correct, and partly to see if the rate varies over time or in relation to other features such as growing budgets). But you also need to "get inside" these organizations and talk to staff (and/or possibly survey them) to try to find out what the internal processes may be that increase or reduce innovativeness.

Combining quantitative and qualitative evidence is therefore often advantageous. But how to do that, in terms of methods, is a whole developing area of its own. The following quotation, taken from an article about how to achieve such synthesis, gives you some idea of the range of techniques:

A range of methods is available for synthesising diverse forms of evidence. These include narrative summary, thematic analysis, grounded theory, meta-ethnography, meta-study, realist synthesis, Miles and Huberman's data analysis techniques, content analysis, qualitative comparative analysis and Bayesian meta-analysis. Methods vary in their strengths and weaknesses, ability to deal with qualitative and quantitative forms of evidence, and types of question for which they are most suitable. (Dixon-Woods et al., 2005, p. 45)

3.4   A menu of methods

There are many ways of classifying methods, and these result in longer or shorter lists depending on how many variations of the basic forms one wishes to include. Table 3.1 borrows from Van Thiel's (2014) excellent introduction to methods and opts for a short, general listing.

One can immediately see how wide the range is. At one end of the spectrum there is close observation of immediate behaviour (or even participation in that behaviour). This observation or participation can be recorded in a number of different ways, ranging from unstructured, impressionistic notes to highly structured counting of various defined behaviours. At the other pole, the scholar may be sitting alone at a desk performing statistical analysis to see what general lessons may emerge from dozens or hundreds of previous studies (meta-analysis).

Methods may be very narrow or very broad. At the narrow end there may be a particular statistical test that performs just one job in one specified set of circumstances. At the broad end there may be whole families of methods which share some common purpose or character. These families are sometimes called "approaches" or "methodologies" rather than methods. Case studies would be one example, comparative analysis another.

3.5   Literature reviews

This is fundamental in most PM research – indeed, it is usually the first step. Without a literature review the researcher may be doomed to repeat work already done and proclaim findings already found. Some scholars view literature reviews principally as ways of shaping a theoretical framework, but in practice many reviews perform other

Table 3.1   Main PM research methods

Method	Approach	Variants	Strategies
Observation	Watching behaviour or listening to talk	Hidden, open, participant	Case study or experiment
Questionnaire	Posing carefully prepared questions, usually to more than one person (sometimes to thousands)	Written, phone, online or face-to-face. Questions can be closed or open or a mixture	Case study or survey or experiment
Interview	Face-to-face questions (also opportunity to observe behaviour and surroundings)	Open-ended, semi-structured, tightly structured. Can be done in the office or on the screen	Case study or survey or narrative analysis
Content analysis	Interpreting the contents of texts (documents, speeches etc.)	Can be done in more or less structured ways. Can be aided by content analysis software	Case study or desk research
Secondary analysis	Reanalysing existing quantitative data	Statistical analysis	Desk research
Meta-analysis	Making an overview (usually quantitative) of the results of relevant previous research	Thematic ordering. Often with statistical analysis	Desk research

Note: Extensively adapted from Van Thiel (2014, table 5.2, p. 59).

functions as well. They can, for example, distil highly relevant data that has already been collected by others and can be used again. They can help bring out what the principal points of academic controversy and disagreement may be. They can reveal gaps and blank spaces – aspects of the topic where little or no work yet appears to have been done. Yet, perhaps because of its very ubiquitousness, the literature review sometimes features little, or not at all in the methods textbooks.

In PM, scholarly journals increasingly insist on literature reviews. If a paper is submitted to any of the top journals dealing with, say, accountability, performance management, partnerships or trust, it is likely to be rejected if the author(s) does not show that she or he has read and understood the latest literature. As a journal editor I used to see 150–200 manuscripts a year, and "the author has not adequately reviewed the literature" was one of the most common criticisms by reviewers. Indeed, literature reviews are themselves a recognized category of article – not the most original and earth-shaking form perhaps, but extremely useful to the rest of us who want to catch up, but don't really have the time to read everything at source. More generally, one mark of a real professional is that she or he knows what is going on in their own sub-field. Professionals are up-to-date in reading their peers. Without this, it is feared, academia would just go round in circles, with no cumulation of knowledge, but rather individuals here and there repeatedly reinventing identical or very similar ideas. (The bad news is that it is perfectly possible to be up-to-date with what is being written and still go round in circles.)

None of this is new, so what is the problem? One problem is that some academics review the literature in a sloppy or inadequate way. They may be biased, they may not look widely enough, they may misunderstand or draw unjustified conclusions from their reading. Another problem is that government reports and policy documents on specific public management issues frequently fail to take any notice at all of available and relevant academic publications. Yet both these problems have been around for a long time.

In addition, however, there are at least two newer challenges:

1. The explosion of writing on PM since the 1980s means that there is far more material to be reviewed. There are more journals, more conferences and more papers than ever before – all this amplified by the increasing pressures, in many countries, for academics to publish.
2. The development of the internet, and the availability of specialist search engines, are tremendously helpful in enabling the individual scholar to track down most of this flood of material, but at the same time internet searching poses new perils and temptations of its own.

These two problems are quite closely inter-related. New technologies have made it far easier to publish – both in hard copy and, especially, electronically. So there are more journals and more issues of some existing journals. This increased flow is powered partly by the accelerating globalization of English as the language of science but even more by the pressures on academics in a lengthening list of countries to "publish or perish". Decisions to appoint academic staff, to promote them and to give them tenure are increasingly made with reference to bibliometric measures such as publication rates, citation rates, impact factors and so on. Whole units and departments are similarly judged, and receive increased or decreased budgets accordingly.

Faced with this flood, one technique that has become popular is the meta-analysis. Originally used in the health sciences, it has expanded its domain into other sectors. In some countries and sectors, it has also become an influential component of policymaking and regulation. As meta-analysis has moved into new territories, it has altered its form, and become less narrowly statistical. In PM one could say that a classic medical-type meta-analysis would usually be impossible – there are simply not enough studies which use a similar statistical method to be able to aggregate and average their findings. However, there are other forms which are more readily applicable to PM, although they still require plenty of hard work. Realist synthesis (see Pawson, 2013) is one of the more powerful of these.

Let us now look more closely at the scale of the problem. If we use Google Scholar to search for references relating to some of the typical PM topics, this is what (on 9 June 2015) was found:

- "performance management" = 4.11 million results
- "public accountability" = 1.30 million results
- "trust in government" = 1.86 million results.

The problem is obvious – how is the scholar to decide what to pay attention to, and what to throw away? It is just not possible to read a million sources – not even if one is fortunate enough to be able to call on the services of a couple of doctoral researchers. The old idea that the professor is someone who has read everything relevant in the field is effectively dead. The professor would be working hard if she or he had even read 1 per cent of the abstracts! Let us therefore consider some of the available methods for thinning the forest so that we can see the trees:

- selection by the research question(s)
- selection by theoretical perspective
- selection by method
- selection by contextual similarity

- selection by reputation of source
- selection by date of publication.

Selection by research question is by far the most respectable and effective approach to selection. To begin with, it obliges academics to *have* a research question, and not just to write vague "about this topic" types of paper. It enables the researcher to focus sharply on "what is relevant and what is not for answering this particular question?". This is usually a much smaller and more easily identified subset than the looser "what is relevant to this subject?".

Selection by theoretical perspective may also be perfectly sensible, especially if the research question is to do with testing/evaluating a particular theory. Then we would want to select all those publications which use or discuss that theory – or some subset of these. However, one problem in doing this in PM is that many papers do not actually declare their theoretical allegiance by name. In other words, as was explained in Chapter 2, some papers may be using theory X but not saying so. However, selection by theoretical perspective can be used on its own, or as a subsiduary partner criterion to selection by research question.

Selection by method was particularly obvious as meta-analyses became more popular in healthcare. Basically, only randomized clinical trials (RCT) which used certain statistical procedures were allowed into the pool of studies to be meta-analysed. Studies which used other methods were excluded as falling below the RCT "gold standard". De facto, this excluded almost all social science studies of healthcare. A number of strong criticisms have been made of this kind of narrowness. Most obviously, it excludes a wide range of academic work which many people find insightful and persuasive. One can also criticize the classic RCT as being a method that tells what leads to what, but fails to explain why that is so (that is, it does not identify the causal processes/ mechanisms that cause the outcomes – see Pawson, 2006). But medical professionals who trust only RCTs are not the only groups to select by method. Within PM we can see some sharp divisions between different camps – such as those who will only recognize de-centred narratives, or those who insist that anything which is "positivist" must be avoided at all costs, or those who will only work with material in a hypothetical-deductive format. One problem with all such excluding filters is that they reduce cognitive dissonance by ensuring that the researcher will seldom face anything which really challenges their own approach (because that is the only place they are willing to look). This is a local instance of the great and ongoing struggle between different ontologies and epistemologies. Within this vast swamp of issues lies the one concerning the most appropriate methods for qualitative approaches in the social sciences. Should they be very similar to those used by quantitative positivists, wholly different or overlapping (see Devers, 1999)? This is a question that faces anyone who wants to undertake a PM literature search based on methodological selection criteria.

Selection by contextual similarity is perhaps a more subtle approach, and it is quite often used – albeit sometimes in a rather loose and unarticulated way. So, for example, if you are interested in the impacts of performance management in Denmark, you may also want to look at material on the impacts of performance management in Sweden or the Netherlands, but probably not at stuff about the impacts of performance management in China or Tanzania. These latter two contexts are just too hugely different to make any sensible parallels viable. Contextual similarity can be used in addition to other criteria. However, it should be noted that the notion of context is itself quite complex (Pollitt, 2013a).

Selection by reputation can be implemented either according to author, or according to source, or both. Thus one might read anything by certain well-known professors but not by academic lesser lights. Or one might focus exclusively on the top five PM journals as measured by Impact Factor (that is, citations), or some other convenient metric. The dangers are obvious. One can easily miss the brilliant article by a young, up-and-coming researcher, or one published in a journal further down the Social Science Citation Index (SSCI) impact rank order. Furthermore, in PM books are sometimes key sources, so the use of bibliometrics to sort out journal articles is only accessing part of the relevant stock of knowledge.

Selection by date usually involves imposing a cut-off point so that no publications more than 3/5/10 years old will be considered. The weakness of this approach is fairly blatant. It assumes that the most recent material is the most valuable and relevant, thus missing insights and lessons from further back (for the extent of this fallacy, see Pollitt, 2008).

One final problem deserves recognition. Many research projects in PM involve, naturally enough, key concepts in the field – such as accountability, performance, governance, networks, partnerships, quality, transparency and so on. The problem is that many of these concepts are somewhat promiscuous. Alternative definitions and interpretations abound. That means that a simple word search may throw up many articles that appear to be about the same thing, but actually are not. Unfortunately (and time-consumingly) literature searchers have to read through all the selected papers to check that these "magic concepts" are being used in tolerably similar ways (often they are not). Software cannot do this for you. Often, this time-heavy step is simply neglected.

Whatever selection tools are used, tackling the electronic mountain of currently available text is often going to exceed the time available to any single individual. More and more of the PM research published in top journals comes from groups of authors, or from members of large research teams working on big, funded projects. Again, this is not necessarily a matter for rejoicing – but it is a fact of life. The implication of this which is significant here is that the literature search may well be carried out by one researcher – often quite a junior one – on behalf of a larger network or team. If this is the case then one conclusion to be drawn from the above analysis is that this person needs to be very carefully briefed indeed. Just to say, "Go and check the literature on accountability" (to take an extreme example) would be radically inadequate. The design of the review and the selection criteria to be applied are a prime topic for collective discussion by the team. What is more, they may need to be adjusted and revised as the search moves forward. Quite frequently the early stages of a review may throw up issues which require reconsideration.

3.6 Statistical analysis

Public administration scholars undertook very little statistical analysis 50 years ago. Over the past two or three decades it has become much more common. A sign of its growing importance is the inclusion of statistical analysis as an unquestioned element in the curricula for PM graduate training courses. In some of the leading PM journals a majority of published articles now contain some form of statistical analysis.

In practice, statistical analysis tends to be associated with a realist ontology and a positivist epistemology. That is, it is most frequently employed by scholars who believe we can find measures that adequately represent aspects of external reality, and that, furthermore, in those measures we will sometimes find patterns that will enable us to confirm or falsify our theoretical hypotheses, or which will suggest new hypotheses that can subsequently be tested. In this way a body of generalizations about inter-relationships can be built up, which will eventually give us a tolerably stable picture of how the political, social and economic worlds work. Such an approach is not favoured by post-modernists or radical constructivists, who found their insights on interpretation, not measurement. More fundamentally, they reject the whole idea of abstract "variables" which can be detached from context and found to have stable mathematical relationships with other variables. Between these radical anti-statistics groups and the hard-line "quants people" lie probably the majority of the PM community, including moderate social constructivists, realists, historians and those who do not espouse a single theory but simply seek to explain and/or understand aspects of their subject. This majority uses and/or welcomes statistical analysis when it seems to offer valid help in solving the research questions being posed, but does not regard it as the be-all-and-end-all of social science.

There are many specific statistical techniques which may be of use, and the number and sophistication of these is expanding all the time. Unless you are yourself highly qualified in statistics you should seek expert advice before choosing a specific technique. Much depends on the particular research question and on the type of data that are likely to be available/collectable.

One interesting development in recent years has been an increase in using experimental methods in PM. Experiments usually involve statistical analysis in which the results of an intervention with a "treatment" group is compared with a "control" group that has not received the treatment. It used to be thought that for a variety of theoretical, ethical and practical reasons, experiments had little scope in PM. Now some scholars are contesting that – arguing that, in principle, experimental approaches can be applied to quite a wide range of circumstances. If you are interested in this you could begin by reading Blom-Hansen et al. (2015), which introduces a special issue of *International Public Management Journal* on experiments in PM.

If one looks at the types of statistical analysis currently being deployed in PM journals and books there are at least three techniques which deserve mention here (for useful introductions, see Robson, 2002, pp. 391–454; Van Thiel, 2014, pp. 118–37). A short introduction cannot teach you how to actually use these techniques, so what follows is no more than the briefest description of what they do. Furthermore, we leave wholly out of consideration the many necessary tests and checks that are used in statistical analysis to ensure that the findings make sense and are "statistically significant" (itself a controversial notion – see Robson, 2002, pp. 400–2). At any event, our three chosen techniques are:

- multiple regression analysis
- factor analysis
- structural equation modelling.

Multiple regression analysis is a procedure for testing whether there are linear relationships between a dependent variable (let us say increases in the government budgetary allocation to healthcare) and two or more independent variables (say the number of minutes of TV news devoted to healthcare issues over the previous year, or the measured incidence of serious health problems such as cancers, heart attacks, strokes and so on). A positive linear relation would mean that as the amount of TV news time increased, so did the subsequent budget allocation – or that as the incidence of life-threatening diseases increased, so did the healthcare budget allocation. Thus this sort of analysis could help confirm or disconfirm the theories that politicians increased budgets when problems were in the news, and that they increased them when indicators of the need for care (that is, serious illnesses) increased. One key result from a multiple regression is the multiple coefficient of determination or R^2. It expresses the proportion of the variance in the dependent variable that is explained by the independent variables in the equation. Therefore, if the R^2 for government budgetary allocations to healthcare is 0.42, then 42 per cent of the variance in healthcare budget increases is positively correlated with the level of TV news coverage and the incidence of serious illnesses. Clearly, if this were a real rather than a fictional example one would wish to take the analysis further in order to ascertain how much of the variance was associated with what might (normatively) be thought to be a weak reason for budget increases (TV news coverage) and how much with a stronger reason (changes in the pattern of actual illnesses).

However, there are at least two important limitations to this kind of analysis. First, the finding of a linear association between the dependent and the independent variables is a correlation, not a cause. It does not prove a causal link, and it certainly does not tell you how such a causal link (if there is one) works. Second, a regression does not tell you whether there are any other independent variables that may be as strong or stronger candidates for explaining the budget changes. For example, it could be that one cause of healthcare budget increases was the powerful lobbying of the medical and nursing professions.

Factor analysis is a procedure for sorting out multiple correlations between variables. Unlike multiple regression analysis it does not seperate out the dependent variable – all variables have equal status (Robson, 2002, p. 433). All the variables are put into a matrix and the factor analysis then identifies clusters of variables which are highly intercorrelated. These then become "factors", thus simplifying the analysis. Factor analysis is used as an exploratory technique. It allows the researcher to move from great complexity (hundreds of correlations) towards manageable simplicity (a few groups of factors). These factors can then, in effect, become a new but much smaller set of variables for further analysis. The example Van Thiel (2014, p. 133) gives is political leadership, where this factor is a construct based on a number of highly correlated variables, including charisma, background and management style.

Structural equation modelling (SEM) is a technique used to confirm (or falsify) hypotheses. It combines aspects of multiple regression and factor analysis. A hypothesized model is tested against all the variables to see what is its "goodness of fit". If the fit is good, the model can be accepted as a reasonable provisonal account of the relationships in question. SEM has become increasingly popular, in PM and other social science fields, for the analysis of non-experimental (real-world) data.

One real life illustration of statistical analysis will have to suffice. Meier and O'Toole are among the acknowledged masters of statistical analysis in PM. In particular, they have published a series of studies based on analysis of the records of the Texas school districts, which have the advantage of bringing together data on personnel characteristics, management practices and student test results. The particular study chosen here is one of the effects of personnel stability on school performance (O'Toole and Meier, 2003). The authors build not one model/equation, but a series of models, explaining the reasons for each analytic move as they go along. These models are fed with data on many variables. For example, they include ten different measures of student and school performance, most importantly pass rates in the Texas Assessment of Academic Skills (TASS). They also have a number of variables representing personnel stability, quality of management and environmental factors. The authors supplemented data from the Texas Education Agency with their own survey. Their model of management quality is "autoregressive, nonlinear, and contingent" (O'Toole and Meier, 2003, p. 48) so they are able to examine many aspects of the interrelationship between their variables, including lagged effects over time.

The overall finding is that personnel stability (both of classroom teachers and school superintendants) *does* have significant and positive effects on educational outcomes. In their own words:

> The findings regarding stability are persuasive in a number of respects. They are unambiguous on the most salient performance indicator, persist in analysis of many other measures of performance, and can even be documented in most autoregressive estimations. Further, the examination of interactions among the independent variables of management and stability . . . indicates that not only do the variables matter, the relationships among them are nonlinear and complex. The model contends that management actions are likely to be contingent on stability. The empirical evidence suggests that the impact of management actions on performance is likely to be contingent on the full range of management decisions and how the various features interact. (O'Toole and Meier, 2003, pp. 60–61)

This then is an example of how sophisticated statistical analysis can deliver not simply a number or a plus or minus in the direction of a relationship, but can be used to tease out interactions between groups of variables, and to suggest new theoretical ideas for further investigation.

3.7   Surveys

An examination of four leading PM journals between 2001 and 2010 showed that the proportion of articles using quantitative methods increased (although predominantly qualitative articles were still in the majority – 56 per cent to 44 per cent – Groeneveld et al., 2015). Within the quantitative group, surveys were the most frequently used method. It is also a method that has become much easier to implement with the growth of the internet. One no longer has to lick many stamps and mail thousands of envelopes and await responses. Surveys can often be carried out quickly, cheaply and effectively by email or telephone.

The (relative) ease with which surveys can be carried out is, however, a temptation. If it is often straightforward to launch a survey it is by no means so easy to ensure that the results will be worth using in a research publication. The literature on survey methods list many pitfalls, including:

- Is the sample representative (of citizens as a whole, senior civil servants, IT specialists or whatever is the unit of analysis in the research in question)?
- Is the response rate going to be high enough? If you survey Directors General (DGs) in country X and get 5 responses out of a population of 47, then there probably isn't much you can say about DGs. There tend to be very different response rates in different organizations and administrative cultures, which can unbalance comparative surveys.
- Did the respondents understand the questions in the same way as you intended? This may be a relatively straightforward thing to check if you are working in your own language, with organizations you already know well. But it becomes more and more difficult to be sure about this the less you know about an organization and/or the more you undertake comparative research, working across several languages.
- Did the respondents have enough information to answer the questions rationally? For example, if you sample all civil servants and ask whether a particular recent reform has been successful some of the respondents will be close to that reform and know about it while others will not. The latter may have opinions, but no first-hand knowledge.
- Were there reasons why one could expect bias in the responses? For example, surveys in a number of countries have indicated that senior officials have had more positive views of the results of recent management reforms than rank-and-file operational staff. This has probably been because (a) the top officials were responsible for creating and designing the reforms (and therefore have a vested and reputational interest in them) and (b) the operational staff see all the day-to-day practical snags and inconveniences of the reforms in a way that top officials do not.

One example of a survey forming the core of an important piece of PM research is Kelman's 2005 book *Unleashing Change: A Study of*

Organizational Renewal in Government. Kelman describes and theorizes a reform in US federal government procurement under President Clinton during the 1990s. He argues that the widespread assumption that civil servants usually resist reform (and therefore have to be punished or rewarded in order to get them to accept it) is wrong. Instead, using a mixture of theories derived from social psychology and innovation research, he develops an alternative model in which support for reform can snowball within the implementing organizations if the reformers encourage and allow a range of internal positive feedback processes by which most staff will eventually convince themselves that the changes are worthwhile. Thus, as time goes by, more and more support for the reform will be "unleashed". Top management does not have to bully or browbeat the rank and file – they will come to see the value of change themselves.

In support of this model Kelman applies statistical inference techniques (including regression analysis) to the findings of two surveys. The first was a survey of contracting staff from 19 federal buying offices (n = 1593) and the second was a series of semi-structured interviews with 272 managers and front line employees. The first survey asked questions about work experiences and contained a number of questions about staff attitudes to the reform (it was a very long questionnaire, having more than 400 questions). It had a very high response rate, probably because it was carried out as an in-house exercise with the support of local office bosses. Most academic surveys of public service staff could not even hope for those levels of response.

The book is well worth reading as an example of how survey results can be used to test or elaborate detailed theoretical predictions. The detailed sense it gives of how the reform developed and was consolidated over time is rare and valuable. Of course it is not perfect. Some commentators were worried about technical aspects of the regression analysis, and about the fact that the survey was asking staff to recall what their attitudes had been a number of years earlier (Hill, 2006). It was also the case, as Kelman acknowledges, that the author and main interviewer, although subsequently a Harvard professor, had himself been a key member of the reform team. Thus he would presumably have been known by many of those involved in the survey. So this was not the standard "outside academic coming in and running a survey" exercise.

3.8   Interviews

Interviews are a very popular and extremely flexible method of gathering information in PM research. Interviews may form the main spine of a research project, or they may come first, as an exploratory phase, or they may come last as a means of probing the meaning of statistical results derived from a survey. Interviewing may be directed at politicians and top officials, at street-level staff or at middle managers. It may be conducted in a highly structured way with a limited number of precise, identical questions (in which case it is almost like a face-to-face survey), or it may be semi-structured (a combination of some core, fixed questions with other more particular and varying questions), or it may be free-form and spontaneous. The more "free" the form, the bigger the trouble in ensuring reliability – which is a major concern for orthodox social scientists (Van Thiel, 2014, pp. 93–4). Interviews may occur as part of a process of research by participant observation, or as seperately arranged meetings, or by telephone. They may be recorded (with the interviewee's permission) or written down as notes. Special advice is available on how to conduct interviews with – for example – political elites, mental health patients, using feminist principles and in a wide variety of other situations. Interviews, therefore, are one example of a method that can be and has been used with a very broad range of theoretical approaches.

There is definitely a craft element to interviewing (Brinkman and Kvale, 2015). I have worked with some research assistants who could prise all sorts of confidences and insights out of their interviewees and others who came back from very similar interviews with nothing but dull platitudes. Of course the first step in interviewing is to obtain access (agreement) and that certainly has a craft aspect (see Section 3.13).

Choosing useful questions is at the heart of successful interviewing. The questions need not only to be closely related to one's research questions, but also to be intelligible to the interviewees. Achieving that is not always as simple as it sounds – civil servants and politicians do not always understand or give the same meaning to commonplace academic terms such as "performance", "accountability", "political" or "governance". Often a few pilot interviews will be beneficial in revealing weaknesses and ambiguities in the questions before the main interview programme is launched. The order of questions is also important. The usual advice is to ask simple, neutral questions first, so as to "settle" the interviewee and, if possible, establish a rapport. Big, awkward, sensitive issues can come later. An elementary, but common, error is to have too many questions for the time available. If you have an hour for an interview and you go in with 15 questions you are already in trouble (unless they are unusually short and simple questions – in which case, why are you asking them?).

The ethics of interviewing is another aspect that cannot be ignored (see also Section 3.13). If you are asking people to talk about sensitive issues which affect their work and/or the reputation of their employing organization you need to be absolutely sure that they and you have a common understanding of what you will, and will not, do with the resulting interview record. Achieving such shared understandings becomes more difficult as one moves to comparative research, and interviews with individuals from different administrative cultures, who speak different languages (see Section 3.1).

For more than a very small number of interviews, prior thought needs to be given not only to the questions themselves but to how answers will be coded and, subsequently, analysed. Fortunately there are a number of pieces of software to help with this. Since these are constantly being updated and improved I will not pick out specific ones here. Without such planning it is all too easy – even with only a couple of dozen interviews – to find oneself lost in a bog of papers and/or audio recordings, unable to give this mass of material sensible form.

Perhaps the final thing to say in this overview is that interviews can be tremendous fun! Not infrequently, they yield new facts, fresh insights or memorable phrases. However, part of the interviewer's craft is not to be unduly drawn in by the one interviewee who has very colourful phrases, or who appears to be willing to reveal hidden secrets. The occasional vivid performance should be set within a perspective on the body of interviews as a whole.

3.9   Case studies

For 30 years or more case studies have probably been the single most frequently published type of PM article (Raadschelders and Lee, 2011; Rhodes et al., 1995). They have attracted both praise and criticism. Like other methods they can be executed well or badly. At the applied/ practitioner end of PM case studies appear to have the advantage that they are usually readily accessible (without mastery of advanced statistical techniques or abstruse conceptual vocabulary). They can also often be carried out quite quickly. Against these advantages, it should be noted that the drawing of broad normative generalizations from one or a few cases may be the single most common – and most damaging – of methodological errors.

We can begin with an orthodox social science view, taken from one of the most influential methods books of the past quarter century:

> Although case-study research rarely uses more than a handful of cases, the total number of observations is generally immense. It is therefore essential to distinguish between the number of cases and the number of observations. (King et al., 1994, p. 52)

This was certainly supportive. However, these authors then went on to place some quite strong restrictions upon the functions and methods of case studies. In essence, they insist that small-N case study research must be conducted on the same basic principles as statistically driven large-N research (that is, research where the academics collect a large number of items of data, such as answers to survey questions from thousands of respondents, or budgetary allocations to different line items over a period of many years). I disagree with this line, since it seems to me to drive all case study work into the fixed strategy/ deductive camp, epistemologically speaking. Case studies then become a kind of second-class citizen in the world of large-N statistical analysis. I prefer what Robson (2002, p. 5) refers to as a "flexible" approach, where we can see a wider range of roles for case studies. Orthodox social science requires a "fixed" approach, with "a very substantial amount of pre-specification of what you are going to do and how you are going to do it" (Robson, 2002, p. 4). In flexible designs, although there is certainly plenty of planning, "much less pre-specification takes place and the design evolves, develops and . . . 'unfolds' as the research proceeds" (Robson, 2002, p. 5). "Flexible" does not mean "shapeless" or "anarchic" – interpretive case studies require a great deal of pre-planning, even if the design may flex as the study proceeds.

High pre-specification is only one of the restrictions which are favoured by the orthodox school. For the main, they also see case studies as having a limited range of functions. First, they have some value in testing existing hypotheses – a single well-chosen and well-specified case (chosen and specified in relation to a defined population of cases to which the relevant hypothesis is supposed to apply) can seriously damage an unreliable hypothesis by showing that it is not confirmed. (Note, though, that the situation is more complicated with probabilistic hypotheses, where one or two counter-cases do not dislodge the original hypothesis. For probabilistic hypotheses, therefore, case studies tend to lose even this function.) Second, in-depth case studies may sometimes serve as useful preliminaries to hypothesis formation. Thus, in a relatively unexplored field, a detailed case may lead the researchers to see what they think may be a causal relationship, which can then be incorporated in a formal hypothesis that can subsequently be tested on a suitably defined large N population.

The past 15 years or so has witnessed a surge of writing about case studies, the main outcome of which can be said to be a much wider appreciation of the range of achievements which can be hoped for from this form of research (Blatter and Blume, 2008; George and Bennett, 2005; Gerring, 2007; Mahoney, 2000; Rueschemeyer, 2003). Blatter and Blume (2008) have advanced a particularly cogent "map" of where case studies can make a contribution. They write of three main approaches to "case studying", each linked to a different epistemology:

- "Co-variance", which looks to confirm or falsify correlations between dependent and independent variables. This comes from the "variables paradigm" we discussed above, and the function of the case is to show whether and how the postulated independent variable(s) produces the (dependent) outcome(s).
- "Causal process tracing", which aims to follow the mechanisms that lead from prior conditions and interventions through to outcomes. This holds out the potential to "get behind" the statistical correlations of the orthodox school and see into the "black box". It embraces a wider notion of "causes" than the "variables paradigm" would normally allow (Kurki, 2008, chapter 6). If a researcher is using a case/cases to trace processes, then the kinds of observations she or he will be pursuing and collecting will be those which show quite detailed steps that lead from cause to consequence. For example, we might be interested in the details of how the UK government's adoption of the 1976 Resource Allocation Working Party formula for the distribution of financial resources between National Health Service (NHS) districts across the UK meant that it was very hard for some districts ever to receive a large increment to their budgets. This was because there were always other districts which were calculated as being "more deserving". Central government could

not easily make exceptions because once the whole issue was embedded in a centralized, national system, any "special deals" would call forth demands and protests from the many other districts that could argue that they had a strong case for reasons that lay outside the formula.

- "Congruence analysis", where the researcher is comparing, on the one hand, a set of expectations that can be deduced from theories and concepts with, on the other, whatever empirical findings emerge from the case(s). This is not the same as the formal hypothesis testing of the variables paradigm. Here theory is treated as an interpretive framework (mild constructivism). The case study is at its most powerful when a plurality of theoretical expectations can be tested against it. When used in this mode, the most valuable observations are not those which would best enable process tracing, but rather those which help the researcher to discriminate between two or more competing theories. For example, in the case of the historical institutionalist comparison of Belgium and the UK mentioned in Chapter 2, Section 2.5, it was found that the theoretical expectation that the fragmented and consensual Belgian political system would be slower and less decisive was confirmed in the case of police policy at the national level, but disconfirmed as far as hospital policy at the local level was concerned (Pollitt and Bouckaert, 2009). This usefully drew attention to another dimension of the contrast between the two different political systems – that even if the fragmented and consensualist Belgian system was slower-moving overall, its unpredictability and lack of national "standardization" meant that local breakthroughs and projects stood a better chance than in the grindingly bureaucratic UK NHS. There were perhaps more "interior windows of opportunity" than in the more majoritarian and centralized system.

Blatter and Blume's reappraisal of case studies is of considerable relevance to PM research. They show that a wider appreciation of the nature of theory coupled with a more plural concept of causation makes the small-N problems identified by the orthodox school look less important and less constraining. If you wish to look at different ways in which case studies can be used you could look at some of the references which have already been cited in this book. Thus, both the examples given in Chapter 2, Section 2.5 were case studies (Pollitt and Bouckaert, 2009; Sundström, 2006). A fascinating read which adopts a more radical approach to narrative is Flyvbjerg's study of the Aalborg project, a town centre redevelopment plan in an old north Danish town. This plan won an award, and was used as a recommended model for the OECD. However, in the end something quite different from the original announced intention happened:

> The Aalborg Project may be interpreted as a metaphor of modern politics, modern administration and planning, and of modernity itself. The basic idea of the project was comprehensive, coherent and innovative, and it was based on rational and democratic argument. During implementation, however, when idea met reality ... It disintegrated into a number of disjointed sub-projects, many of which had unintended, unanticipated, and undemocratic consequences. (Flyvbjerg, 1998, p. 225)

This is an exciting story, well worth attention not only for its intrinsic interest, but also for the twin narrative strategy pursued by the author.

3.10   Textual analysis

PM academics study organizations which perform public functions, and some of the main outputs of public organizations are texts. These include laws, regulations, budgets, policy statements, public management reform documents, explanatory leaflets, organizational websites, letters, emails and so on. Many insights can be gained by close study of these texts, and how they change from one government or organizational regime to the next (for example, how the contents and appearance of annual reports shift over time). One can also study public reactions to specific texts – how far can the public understand their tax forms or the statements they receive from their local authorities explaining how local budgets are being spent, or the consent forms they are asked to sign when about to undergo certain surgical procedures? How easy or difficult is it for the public to use particular public websites?

There is no one best way of studying a text. Some methods are predominantly quantitative, others qualitative. Some are very formal and fixed, others flexible and interpretive. Some count words (how has the frequency of terms like "governance", "transparency" and "partnership" changed over time?). Others attempt to identify the range of narratives generated by particular groups in particular organizations (Bevir and Rhodes, 2006; Pollitt, 2013b). Texts are by no means necessarily "on the page" – they may be spoken or acted out (Borins, 2011 offers an interesting analysis of governing narratives in films and TV series). As usual, much depends on the precise research question or questions being posed, and on the theoretical perspective(s) within which the work is being conducted (see Section 3.2).

One good example of textual analysis was Smullen's 2010 book *Translating Agency Reform: Rhetoric and Culture in Comparative Perspective*. Noting the existence of an international fashion for creating semi-autonomous executive agencies, Smullen set out to explore what had been written and said about these reforms in three countries – Australia, the Netherlands and Sweden. Her theoretical approach combined a particular theory of rhetoric with grid group cultural theory (GGCT). GGCT is borrowed from anthropology and sociology and has been used by a number of PM scholars (for example, Hood, 1998). In each country she sought expert advice on what the key agency documents and speeches had been and, having selected these, applied her analytic tools to these texts. Her findings were that agency reforms were discussed in very different terms in each of the three countries and languages. Furthermore the very styles of speech (rhetoric) that were held to be most persuasive varied from country to country. Other research had already demonstrated that the agencies themselves varied a good deal: for example, in legal status, budgetary and personnel authority and informal relationships with the centre of government. Smullen's work showed that, on top of these "real" differences, the whole discussion and argumentation around agencies tended to be highly country-specific. In other words, any thought that the international trend to agencies was some uniform process, with similar arguments being deployed, similar organizational forms being created and similar results being achieved could not be further from the truth.

3.11 Comparisons

International comparative work has been a growth sector in academic PM. There was little of it in the 1950s and 1960s but now it is a recognized sub-field with its own journals and conferences. One partial explanation of this would be the advent of the internet and of cheap and easy international travel, both of which have made it much easier for academics to communicate across national boundaries and to travel to do research in other countries. There is also a sense in which the wider processes of globalization have pushed many academics – in many social science subjects not only PM – to realize that they cannot fully understand what is going on inside their countries unless they also know something of what is going on outside it.

What does a public administration study have to have before it qualifies as "comparative"? The potential range is wide. At one end one has the seasoned analysis of the senior civil service in country X which, towards the conclusion, hazards a few speculative remarks about how things are different in countries Y and Z. At the other end there are massive statistical exercises which compare hundreds of variables across dozens, or even hundreds, of countries, but give little, if any, flavour of individual countries.

Here I take the rough and ready view that to qualify for the label "comparative" the book or paper has to have comparison as a prime purpose rather than a subsidiary element or afterthought. Furthermore, I follow the conventional assumption that the phrase "comparative public administration" refers primarily to comparisons between nation states. Note that I mean comparisons *between*, not just comparisons *of*. Thus I certainly include here comparisons between particular institutions within specified states (ombudsmen, budgets, the senior civil service and so on) as well as comparisons of whole systems. It should be clearly acknowledged, however, that many of the pleasures and problems of inter-country comparison also apply, in full or part, to comparisons between sub-national and supra-national identities. Comparing US states, for example, has been a considerable industry within American PM. The same is true for comparing local authorities in a number of European countries. Comparing cases is a feature of a lot of PM writing, in many countries. More recently comparing international institutions has become a budding sub-field. International organizations have come to play very important roles in the spread of PM ideas and practices. Transnational networks, often organized and led by inter-governmental organizations (IGOs) such as the OECD or World Bank, define, circulate, legitimate and in some cases monitor the application of new management processes and techniques. One important implication of this is that simple comparisons of what nation states are doing may miss much of the story. Increasingly, comparativists need to incorporate a transnational as well as an international dimension to their analyses.

Do PM publications need to have any particular theoretical or methodological apparatus in order to be classified as "comparative"? I provisionally answer "no". Comparison is comparison: it can be exe-cuted well or badly, by multiple regression analysis or semiotic analy-sis, by a series of vivid descriptive case studies or a systematic listing of expenditures per capita, or by a host of other devices. The degree to which explicit discussion of theories and methods of comparison plays a part also varies. In quite a few comparative publications the authors just go right ahead and make comparisons, without any overt theo-retical or methodological baggage whatsoever. For example, an edited collection entitled *Comparative Administrative Change and Reform* contains hardly any discussion of alternative approaches to compari-son, although containing plenty of "meat" (Pierre and Ingraham, 2010). In other works, however, the reader is treated to long theoretical and methodological preambles (for example, Peters, 1996).

If, however, comparisons can be undertaken in so many different ways, is comparison really a method? It is true that there is and has been a kind of "standard scientific model" for comparison, and that has been the hypothetico-deductive approach. Here one chooses a level and a unit of analysis, one specifies a hypothesis constructed around sets of independent and dependent variables, one gathers data on the largest possible number of cases and one applies the appropriate statistical techniques to investigate correlations (for example, the enormously influential Lijphart, 1999). Any basic textbook on comparative meth-odology will spell out how to do this. Lijphart's analysis offers us a cor-relation matrix of the ten variables distinguishing majoritarian from consensus democracies in 36 democracies (Lijphart, 1999, p. 244). It does not matter much than no one could be an "expert", in a thick description sense, of 36 countries – as long as the correlation matrix can be filled, the orthodox view is that conclusions can be drawn.

Comparisons of smaller numbers of countries are, from this perspec-tive, more difficult but still potentially valuable. Orthodox/mainstream researchers are still in the business of specifying hypotheses that connect independent and dependent variables, but the problems of holding all other things equal become more challenging. A number of orthodox texts discuss small N comparisons in terms of two tech-niques which were originally proposed in the mid nineteenth century by John Stuart Mill: the "most similar systems design" (MSSD) and the most different systems design" (MDSD). With MSSD one looks at countries which share many features in terms of (potentially) inde-pendent variables but nevertheless produce one or more outcomes (dependent variables) that differ. In short, how can one explain similar countries producing different outcomes? MDSD, by contrast, compares different countries (for example, developing and developed, or dictatorships and democracies) which produce some similar outcomes (Landsman, 2008, pp. 70–82 gives a useful summary).

However, the domain of the orthodox model seems gradually to be shrinking, as both critique of the model per se and the adoption of a variety of "post-positivist" approaches have weakened its grip. It still has strongholds in particular journals and departments, especially in the USA, but most of the comparative PM that has been published recently does not follow much of this formula (see, for example, the discussion in Pollitt and Bouckaert, 2009, pp. 170–94). Long ago Peters (1996, p. 16) could already observe that "the comparative method (like the principles of any religion) is more bowed to than followed".

With respect to large-scale comparisons, critical realism and mild constructivism come somewhere between the ease of the orthodox and the uncomfortableness or denial of the post-modernists and radical constructivists. On the one hand, critical realists and mild constructivists are cautious about how far across space and time it is plausible to make comparisons. So there would be a reluctance, for example, to compare criminal justice policy in Belgium with criminal justice policy in China. On the other hand, concepts and metaphors do have some portability – they are not strictly confined to one spatio-temporal location. What is important is to ensure that the respective contexts being compared are carefully analysed and, if possible, are not wildly different.

The overall conclusion, however, is that if one analyses not just an abstract variable like "decommodification" or "transparency" but rather looks in detail at the mechanisms and the social frameworks in which they are embedded, then realist or constructivist comparison is quite feasible. One may have to abandon the orthodox ambition to make generalizations about all the countries in the world, or even about any large number of countries, but those generalizations were in any case likely to be pitched at a very high level of abstraction. "Universal mechanisms of change may exist but they are unlikely to yield an intelligible account of specific spatio-temporal contexts" (Kay, 2006, p. 23). Indeed, some of the most widely publicized and ambitious international comparisons, the "World Governance Indicators" from the World Bank, show very clearly what the dangers and limitations of this kind of high-level, large N comparison can be (Pollitt, 2010). Critical realists will look at smaller numbers of cases, but in more depth, and with the specific ambition of understanding contexts as well as mechanisms.

As far as the academic PM community is concerned there is evidently no "one best way" of comparison. However, even if there is no general agreement concerning the most appropriate comparative methods, there is at least a fairly widespread (though not universal) acceptance that certain features of comparison pose difficult problems or choices. Here we will mention just four. First, there is the problem of equivalence: how do we know that phenomena in different countries that go under the same label are actually the same thing? For example, what constitutes "corruption" in one country may not be "corruption" in another (Peters, 1996, pp. 23–5). This problem becomes more acute as the number of languages to be compared grows. Smullen's study of agency policies in Australia, the Netherlands and Sweden (referred to in Section 3.9) found numerous subtle differences in the usage of terms (Smullen, 2010). Second, there is the choice of level of analysis: should we compare whole national systems (for example, Pollitt and Bouckaert, 2011), or specific organizations within systems (for example, the senior civil service – Bekke et al., 1996), or specific organizational processes such as budgeting, or individual-level decision-making (as in some rational choice approaches)? Alternatively, should we make culture our main focus, in which case we can again approach it at different levels: entire systems, or specific organizations, or groups of individuals (Hood, 1998). These are tricky choices because there is usually a trade-off as well as complex linkages between levels. The systems approach may find many specific decisions or policies within a given system which appear to be "exceptions" or "variations". By contrast, an organizational/institutional approach may find that assumed commonalties between organizations turn out to be rather different when understood within the broader (systemic) political or cultural context. Third, once we have agreed on the level of analysis, which units should we pick as our focus? Let us say we have decided on a meso-level, organizational study, comparing ministries of finance, or national audit offices, or ombudsmen, in a number of countries. Should we focus on structures (organigrams and organizational positioning relative to other related organizations), or on processes (how are decisions taken, what are the standard operating procedures), or on actors (what kinds of people with what kinds of attitudes and beliefs are employed in each organization)? Each can produce a very different kind of explanation, and each requires various delicate and nuanced interpretive judgements by the researcher (Aberbach and Rockman, 1987, pp. 482–5). Of course in principle these units of analysis are not mutually exclusive. One could study them alongside one another. In practice, however, the money and time budgets of most research projects are likely to force if not an outright choice, then at least a preferential emphasis. This last comment leads us directly to the fourth problem. Almost every major work in comparative public administration comments on the variability, and in many cases downright absence or unreliability, of data from different countries. Progress is being made in the improvement of international datasets, but it is gradual rather than revolutionary.

To summarize, the range of methods that may be employed to make comparisons is very broad. What, then, is comparison doing here in a methods chapter? My justification comprises several strands. First, comparison is very important within PM and therefore deserves a place *somewhere* in an Advanced Introduction. Second, it certainly doesn't fit in Chapter 2 – it is not a theory. Third, although not one method it could be argued that comparison is a collection of methods (perhaps an "approach") which is aimed, at least in part, at testing theories (the same could be said for case studies and textual analysis – neither actually comprise a single method). In this third sense comparison performs a method-like function. For example, if one wished to test the theory that a market-based healthcare system would be clearly more efficient than a centrally controlled public healthcare system one could compare various national systems. One would find, for example, that the predominantly market-based US healthcare system was vastly more expensive (as a percentage of gross national product (GNP)) than the predominantly state-run UK NHS, yet yielded healthcare outcomes for the American population that were mainly worse or at least no better. Thus comparison would set in train further investigations of why this was so, and what further comparative data might be available from other countries with different mixes of public and private provision.

3.12 Qualitative comparative analysis (QCA)

I have singled QCA out from the main (preceding) section of comparisons because it is relatively novel and seems, at the time of writing, to be "a coming thing" in our field. QCA has been around in political science and public policy studies for more than a quarter of a century, but it is only in the last few years that it has begun to creep into PM publications and doctoral theses.

QCA compares cases or organizations or policies or processes on the basis of *sets* (configurations) of carefully chosen and specified characteristics. These characteristics are presumed to be conditions which may promote or retard certain outcomes – they are therefore characteristics of potential theoretical significance. QCA was originally particularly intended to deal with relatively modest numbers of cases (between 10 and 50) although more recently it has sometimes been adapted for larger *N*s. The cases – or rather the set of characteristics making up each case – are compared using Boolean algebra. Data analysis is both formal and rigorous. The centrepiece of analysis is a truth table which lists all the configurations of conditions and their respective outcomes. From this the most parsimonious set of causes for a specified outcome can be calculated. Nevertheless, QCA is usually referred to as a qualitative technique, and is also sometimes classified as a variety of the case study approach.

QCA focuses on "multiple conjunctural causation" (Berg-Schlosser et al., 2009, p. 8). Outcomes are seen as being caused by different *combinations* of conditions, not by one or two independent variables. So three or four cases with the same outcome may have stemmed from different mixtures of conditions (this is called equifinality). Neither is it assumed that the absence of a particular outcome will necessarily be the result of the reverse of the set of conditions which produce the outcome. The causes of absence may be quite different from the causes of presence – this is termed causal asymmetry (Fiss, 2011). So QCA causal effects are neither uniform nor symmetrical, as they are in, say, a multiple regression analysis (Hudson and Kühner, 2013, p. 283). There is a particular concern with conditions which are necessary or sufficient. Necessary conditions are those which are present in every case where the outcome is found. However, necessary is not yet sufficient – a sufficient condition is one that by itself guarantees the outcome (such powerful causes may not exist in some instances). Conventional cars need both fuel and wheels – both are necessary, but neither by itself is sufficient to get a car on the road.

Many past applications of QCA have been directed to big policy issues, such as the trajectories of welfare states. Smaller-scale applications of particular interest to PM scholars – for example, a regional public health initiative aimed at helping people who were long-term unemployed for health reasons – are only recently beginning to accumulate. Readers are advised to look out issue 32 of the journal *Policy and Society* where they will find a collection of QCA applications and a thoughtful introductory overview of the advantages of QCA as compared with some of the more traditional techniques of statistical analysis (Hudson and Kühner, 2013).

3.13   Access, time and some other practicalities

Most empirical work requires access to public sector organizations (and/or to private sector or civil society associations which are contracted or partnered to provide public services). It also requires time to implement whatever methods are being used and then to analyse the results. These "craft" aspects of PM research deserve a few words of their own.

Access is not a straightforward issue. One might have supposed that the spread (over the past two or three decades) of ideas of "open government" and "transparency" would have made life easier for academic researchers. Well, they have, in some important ways, as certainly has the advent of the Net, and the rapidly expanding opportunities for Net-based research. However, other trends have pushed in the opposite direction, making academic access more difficult, at least in some countries. Such counter-trends have included politicization, mediaization and the bureaucratization of ethics. Another has been the increase in time pressures on many if not most public servants. I now briefly elaborate on each of these.

The increasingly hectic pace of politics, and the increasingly intrusive pressure from the 24/7 media, have often "politicized" hitherto relatively neutral administrative issues. In a number of countries – perhaps especially the USA and the UK – the slightest hiccup with public services is immediately thrown against the relevant politicians, up to and including the prime minister/president. A surgical procedure goes wrong; a school teacher is discovered to have falsified test scores; a child is abused by its parents while officially under the scrutiny of the local social services department – in each case demands may swiftly fall on the government: "Well, minister, what are you going to do to make sure that this never happens again?" In this climate even mundane administrative processes may be seen by their managers as "sensitive", and perhaps too risky to allow academic researchers access to. This sensitivity is accentuated if you are hoping to conduct your interviews or surveys anywhere near an election.

By "the bureaucratization of ethics" I mean the fact that within the past three decades research ethics has become a matter of formal rules and procedure rather than a taken-for-granted. Most universities now have research ethics protocols of one kind or another, as do many professional associations, and quite a few public sector organizations. This is mainly for the good – clients, patients and junior staff have sometimes in the past been subject to academic research where their full understanding and consent may not have been properly obtained. Occasionally, however, it is quite frustrating. I was doing a piece of research into hospital policy where I had approached a number of hospital chief executive officers (CEOs), who had each agreed to be interviewed about their hospitals. But before I could conduct these interviews, my research proposal had to go through the local health authority ethics committee. In one of these I was confronted by a table full of medical doctors, accustomed to dealing with applications by medical researchers for access to patients, on whom they wished to carry our procedures. I was treated as though I was one of these body-snatchers. How could I guarantee that I would not bully and exploit my interview "subjects", they asked me? Well, I said, I was interviewing very powerful managers who earned twice as much as me or more, and would not have agreed to the interview if they hadn't quite fancied it. That was, of course, the wrong answer! I was told that I had to get each of the CEOs to sign a consent form, the wording of which would have to be approved by the ethics committee. The rest of the story goes on too long to be recounted here, but suffice it to say that at least one CEO laughed at the idea of signing anything and then made somewhat derogatory remarks about the ethics committee. Welcome to the real world of PM fieldwork!

Now we come to time pressures on officials. We live in an age of "more for less" – more public services are to be provided by fewer staff, with diminished budgets. Spending an hour or two with an academic researcher now needs to be justified, or justifiable, to one's employing organization. As a junior academic, researching for my PhD I once got to interview an ex-UK Prime Minister at the House of Commons. Having been told by his secretary that I had a maximum of 15 minutes I launched into my questions at hectic speed. The great man smiled indulgently at this nervous haste and asked me to stay for lunch. Two hours later I had answers to all my questions, and much more! Unfortunately this kind of relaxed generosity is now in very short supply. When approaching officials (or politicians) one needs to appre-ciate that they may have very, very little time to spend on something that appears to be of only marginal use to them, or no use at all. Seasoned academic researchers usually develop a variety of tactics for gaining attention and interest. For example, you can specifically mention an issue which you know your interviewee is currently intensely interested in (demonstrating that you actually already know details of their work or problems usually helps establish credibility, and signals that you are not a naive or casual academic wanderer). Or you can mention that you have already had an interview with your interviewee's boss, or with one of his or her rivals in other parts of the organization, or in other organizations (this may tempt them to try to find out what you have been told, or may encourage them to see you in order to make sure that you also hear their side of the story). Or you can point out that your research is being funded by some impressive body such as a National Research Council or the European Commission. There are many other possible "hooks", but you should also resign yourself to the fact that sometimes all the bait in the world is not enough, and your target interviewees simply will not see you.

Now we move on from access to time per se. In an immediate, practical sense time is important to researchers because of a combination of two factors. First, most research projects nowadays have fairly strict time budgets – the research grant lasts two to four years, and by the end of that time material must be written up (and preferably some of it already published). Second, when one tries to "get inside" public organizations it tends to be those organizations, rather than the researcher, that control how long it takes to get things done. If the research is not particularly important for the organization then it will not put it high up its agenda, so interviews, for example, may take a long time to arrange. It is wise to seek access as soon as possible (often this can be done before the research project is finally approved).

There is also a quite different sense in which time is relevant to methods. That is, to put it simply, if your research wishes to explain a development over time (for example, growing budgets, falling morale) then you will need to choose methods that can cope with a longitudinal (diachronic) dimension. This is not always done. Several times I have seen the results of a one-off survey used to try to explain a trend or change over time. But surveys are a cross-sectional (synchronic) method. Of course, one can ask respondents how they compare the status quo with some point in the past, but although this is a lot better than nothing, it is still vulnerable to systematic biases. Psychologists have shown that we continuously adjust our views of the past, and that statements about what we thought about an issue years ago are not necessarily to be trusted. This is called "hindsight bias" (Kahneman, 2012). (This bias is by no means necessarily a matter of conscious deception – respondents may actually think that their view five years ago was different from what records at the time may show it to have been. Those who have been intimately involved in some matter of public import – like a major reform – are probably particularly vulnerable to this rewriting of their personal history of thought.) Historians know that they need to look at contemporary documents to get a sense of a given period – not at what later generations thought might have been the ideas of that period. PM scholars need to learn the same lesson, and to use longitudinal methods and time series data when trying to address questions with a significant time dimension.

The final point is that there is almost always some element of power lurking in PM empirical research (Clegg and Pitsis, 2011). Public organizations (and private ones) are sensitive about their reputations. So are the individuals the researcher may interview or observe. You want something from them, but they also probably want something from you (and I don't necessarily mean anything as crude as active support – there are many kinds of subtle legitimation, or information, which academics can provide). The wise academic will remain continuously alert to this dimension. One is taking part in a "performance": neutral, "scientific" academic on your part, responsible official, dynamic manager or sensitive politician on theirs. Those academics who do not understand this may miss a lot, and misinterpret even more. Or they may simply not gain access at all.

3.14 Concluding observations

In the first section of this chapter attention was drawn to the fact that the PM field was host to two sorts of arguments about methods. First, there were the debates about which methods were best. Second, there was a kind of meta-debate about what prominence to give to methods at all, with some voices suggesting that concerns with methods had become too dominant, and might be unduly restricting the kinds of topics that scholars were willing to tackle. Here at the end of the chapter we might just note that this kind of concern (like many aspects of PM) is far from new. Neither does it come exclusively from postmodernists and radical social constructivists. The following quotation hails from a leading American social scientist writing more than half a century ago:

> Just now, among social scientists, there is a widespread uneasiness, both intellectual and moral, about the direction their chosen studies seem to be taking . . . It is quite frankly my hope to increase this uneasiness, to define some of its sources, and to help transform it into a specific urge to realize the promise of social science, to clear the ground for new beginnings . . . my conception stands opposed to social science as a set of bureaucratic techniques which inhibit social inquiry by "methodological" pretensions, which congest such work by obscurantist conceptions, or which trivialize it by concern with minor problems unconnected with publicly relevant issues. (Wright Mills, 1959 [2000], pp.19–20)

This opinion from C.Wright Mills reminds us that there is a balance to be sought between methodological purity and social and political relevance. The more one insists on some particular brand of the former, the narrower the range of questions one can expect to be able to answer. On the other hand, if one concentrates entirely on addressing questions of high social and political relevance and ignores all the boring technical stuff about methods, then what is there to distinguish one's findings from the opinions of untrained, non-academics? As will be seen in Chapter 4, the PM academic community is both large and diverse, and in some parts of it are temptations to gravitate towards one or the other pole in this spectrum.

3.15   Further reading

I have already made a number of references to *Research Methods in Public Administration and Public Management* (Van Thiel, 2014) and to one of the best broader introductions to social science research – *Real World Research* (Robson, 2002). Both are well worth attention.

There is also a great deal of more specialized advice available on particular approaches and methods. For example, Kline (2011) offers *Principles and Practice of Structural Equation Modelling*. Ruel et al. have produced a useful text on *The Practice of Survey Research: Theory and Applications* (2015). And on the recommended strategy of integrating quantitative and qualitative methods there is Morgan's *Integrating Qualitative and Quantitative Methods: A Pragmatic Approach* (2014). Interviewing is well served by a small library of advisory texts – my choice would be Brinkman and Kvale's *Interviews: Learning the Craft of Qualitative Research Interviewing* (2015) but there are also many more specialized treatments. For case studies there are also many recent commentaries. My own choices would be twofold. First, there is the mainstream "bible", R.K. Yin's *Case Study Research* (5th edition, 2014). A little more adventurous, perhaps, is Blatter and Haverland's *Designing Case Studies* (2012). Flyvbjerg's *Rationality and Power* (1998) provides an absorbing example of a case study with strong theoretical intentions. Textual analysis takes many forms, and I am unaware of a single source that covers all. Reissman's *Narrative Methods for the Human Sciences* (2008) is a good general approach and Bevir and Rhodes's *Governance Stories* (2006) is an example of a narrative approach in action. Comparisons are well discussed in Landman's *Issues and Methods in Comparative Politics* (2007) although the author stays fairly firmly within the bounds of orthodox social science. Applications of comparative analysis to PM can be found in Kuhlmann and Wollmann's *Introduction to Comparative Public Administration* (2014) and Pollitt and Bouckert's *Public Management Reform: A Comparative Analysis* (2011). Finally, for QCA, consult Rihoux and Ragin's *Configurational Comparative Methods: Qualitative Comparative Analysis (QCA) and Related Techniques* (2009).

For those embarking on masters or doctoral theses there are a number of guidebooks which address, inter alia, methods and approaches. I particularly liked Patrick Dunleavy's no-nonsense *Authoring a Ph.D.* (2003).

In conclusion, I should reiterate what most guides say about statistical analysis. You will probably need detailed help – preferably from an expert but also from a guide to the particular software you are thinking of using. There are many of these software packages and accompanying guides, so you will need to track down the ones that cover your particular technique. An obvious example is Field's *Discovering Statistics using IBM SPSS Statistics* (2013). Consult both the guides and the experts earlier rather than later in your research. That will lessen the risk of wasting a great deal of time. And practice with the software to get to know it before running your data for real.

4 The public management community

Academic politics is the most vicious and bitter form of politics because the stakes are so low. (Wall Street Journal, 20 December 1973, quoting the University of Columbia political scientist, Wallace Sayre)

4.1 Introduction

Many introductory texts do not have a chapter – or much material at all – directly descriptive of the community of men and women and organizations that make up the discipline or field. They focus overwhelmingly on subject or disciplinary borderlines, theories, methods and current debates – on the subject matter, somewhat abstracted from the people who study it. However, I tend to believe that anthropological or cultural perspectives are rather useful in explaining much of what happens in the field, and also in sensitizing newcomers to just what kind of a family it is they are getting themselves into.

At the time of writing the field of academic public management is mainly western, mainly male and dominantly Anglophone. Each of these features may well be changing – but more of that in a moment. Universities with a significant presence in the field are not evenly distributed across the western world. The USA remains the single largest community. However, PM, unlike, say, economics or engineering, is not a subject that one can count upon to feature in the profile of almost any university of size and stature. In fact it is wholly absent from some of the top American universities, yet at the same time vigorously active in other top universities, as well as across a range of other types of university. Canada also has a number of active centres. In western Europe PM features prominently in Belgium, Denmark, Finland, Germany, the Netherlands, Norway and the UK, but, although definitely present, is less salient in, say, France, Italy or Sweden. Australia and New Zealand – in some ways "western" – though perhaps decreasingly so – also have universities with strong PM departments and units.

The precise organizational location of PM within those universities where it is studied varies enormously. There are some departments, institutes and units of PM/PA. But there are many other "nests" for PM scholars. Quite often they are housed together with public policy or political science. Frequently they can be found in business schools. Occasionally they may be put into schools of law, or positioned in interdisciplinary units which study climate change or the internet, or the future of the welfare state. This diversity of locations does not prevent, but does not particularly help, PM scholars to feel that they are all part of one community.

Although the above broad pattern has held for several decades there are signs of change. Significant centres of university-level study have developed in East Asia, including China, Japan and South Korea (see, for example, the 2012 special issue of the *International Review of Administrative Sciences*). A few centres have also emerged in Latin America and in the post-Communist states of central and eastern Europe (see, for example, Bresser-Pereira and Spink, 1999; Randma-Liiv et al., 2011). A higher percentage of the younger, up-coming academics are female (PM was a particularly male domain, despite the fact that in many public services in many countries female staff have long outnumbered male staff). A younger generation of female full professors has begun to freight our bookshelves with high quality publications (for example, Kuhlmann and Wollmann, 2014; Mungiu-Pipiddi, 2015; Riccucci, 2010; Van Thiel, 2014). Serious PM journals are being published in, for example, French, Chinese and Spanish, as well as in English. This emergence is somewhat disguised by the fact that the reputational rankings of PM journals are, at the time of writing, still dominated by American surveys (Van de Walle and Van Delft, 2015).

However, this international dominance – sometimes seemingly almost hegemony – of the "Anglosphere" (Wilks, 2013) may well be beginning to falter. The growing economic and political strength of Asia, combined with the very mixed results of many of the PM reform ideas and practices exported from the Anglosphere over the past 20 or 30 years may well make non-western countries considerably less inclined to look up to the latest management fashions emerging from Washington and London (Pollitt, 2015b). The BRICS countries (Brazil, Russia, India, China and South Africa) are likely to gain not only confidence but also more influential positions within those international organizations such as the International Monetary Fund (IMF), World Bank and OECD which sit at the hub of key networks for disseminating management ideas. And a number of these countries – most obviously China – not only possess economic and political clout, but also have long and deep administrative traditions of their own (Cheung, 2012). Anglosphere dominance is unlikely to disappear overnight, but it is hard to see how it will be sustained at past levels over the next few decades.

One indisputable trend has been the internationalization of academic PM. On the one hand, large differences remain between different national communities. One example would be the relative introversion of the large US community and its seeming unwillingness to learn from the Europeans, let alone from other continents (Rhodes, 2010, 2011).

And again, there are still quite deep barriers between the academic communities within Europe. In western Europe consider, say, the groupings in the Mediterranean countries compared with those in Germany, the Nordic countries or the UK. The former have been much less active in European networks than the latter. At international conferences it is still quite common for Francophone workshops to attract one set of participants and Anglophone workshops another – with only limited cross-language traffic. The divisions between eastern and western Europe are perhaps even more profound. Although the central and eastern European states have a thriving academic network (NISPAcee – see www.nispa.sk) the general level of resourcing and training in public management in that region remains very weak (Nemec et al., 2012).

On the other hand, the period since about 1980 has seen the proliferation of various international academic networks, some European, some fully international. More recently we have also witnessed international networks in Latin America and Southeast Asia. All this has, of course, been hugely aided by the growth of the internet (and cheap air travel). International PM conferences, rare events during the 1960s and 1970s, are now numerous, and a substantial community of scholars has grown up working across national and linguistic boundaries. On a personal level, at the beginning of my academic career I knew very few fellow PM scholars outside the UK. Now, when I check my emails, the overwhelming majority of my correspondents are from other countries – north, south, east and west.

4.2   The PM diaspora

The preceding section has described some aspects of the core PM academic community. In this core academics bear titles and work in units whose names include terms like "public management", "public administration" or "government". They read journals the titles of which also incorporate these terms – for example, *Journal of Public Administration Research and Theory*, *Public Administration Review*, *Public Administration*, *Public Management Review* and *Governance*. But it is an unusual feature of PM that many other academics and students also study the subject – or certainly parts of it – without necessarily adopting these terms or thinking of themselves as part of this core. We could call this "non-core" the PM diaspora (although that might be thought provocative in so far as some of these people would not want to recognize PM as their homeland at all). I have never seen an estimate of the total size of this dispersed community, but impressionistically it is probably bigger than the core.

Who am I talking about here? Several different groups. Probably closest to the core are those academics and students studying Development Administration. This is essentially PM for the developing world and has a strong "applied" or practitioner-oriented element. It has a long, though not always entirely honourable, history (Dunsire, 1973, pp. 134–44; Pollitt, 2011). I write "not always entirely honourable" because, at its worst, this part of the academic community has been responsible for disseminating the patronising and simplistic assumption that what the developing world needs is to import "western" (and particularly American) models of institutions and processes. (There is endless evidence that this usually does not work!) At its best, however, development administration has produced nuanced, contextualized accounts of the huge difficulties facing many developing states, and what some useful approaches to these problems might be (for example, Andrews, 2013). Scholars studying development administration are sometimes located in their own units, are sometimes co-located together with PM, and sometimes are to be found in a variety of other academic corners.

Then there are many students and academics concerned with degree programmes in education, nursing, social work or police studies. Included in their curricula will often be modules on organization and management. They may not read the *Journal of Public Administration Research and Theory*, but they will read journals such as *Higher*

Education Quarterly or the *Journal of Health Services Research and Policy* which very frequently contain articles on management issues. They will debate the latest reorganizations in each of these major public services and attend conferences with related themes. It is also the case that many "core" PM staff publish extensively in non-core, specialist journals – one of a number of reasons why simply counting published papers from the core PM journals can easily give a misleading picture of what academics studying PM are actually doing (Van de Walle and Van Delft, 2015).

Another group in the diaspora are public officials themselves. In many countries civil and public servants of various kinds undergo training as an integral part of their professional trajectories. During this training they will usually be exposed to the currently fashionable ideas of management and leadership (Pollitt and Op de Beeck, 2010; Van Wart et al., 2015). Their teachers may come from the core PM community, or from management consultancies, or internally, from the public services themselves. Globally, the total number undergoing such training in any given period almost certainly outnumbers the university students taking core academic PM courses. Of course most of this training cannot be directly compared with university courses in terms of duration or depth – many courses are just a day or two long – but nevertheless in terms of numbers of persons involved this is a major site for PM teaching and learning.

A fourth group would be management consultants. Several of the big, international management consultancies have become major players in the business of advising governments on how to organize and manage (Saint-Martin, 2000). Government work has become an important part of the overall business of firms such as Accenture, Deloitte, KPMG and Price Waterhouse Cooper (see, for example, KPMG, 2013a, 2013b; National Audit Office, 2006). These consultancies are often favoured employment destinations for successful PM graduates. Formally or informally, consultancy staff study the academic PM literature, hunting for useful evidence and ideas. Of course they are by no means confined to this material – they also look at generic management literature, government publications and a number of other sources. Management consultancies have become influential actors in the formulation, circulation and application of new PM ideas and techniques (Sahlin-Andersson and Engwall, 2002).

4.3   Measuring the performance of PM academics

How do academics judge the quality of their own work? In common with many other disciplines, over the past two or three decades PM has witnessed an evolution from a broadly informal/connoiseurial/reputational ranking of the relative status of different individuals and departments to a much more closely measured situation. Rankings are now more numerous, more public and more closely based on various kinds of bibliometric measures. This tendency, which began in the USA, is not universal, but it has become internationally widespread (Lewis, 2014). It is probably more intense in the Anglosphere than elsewhere, but it has already spread quite widely in western Europe, and is also noticable in some Asian universities.

Table 4.1 gives one small example of this kind of exercise. It shows the numbers of articles published in Social Science Citation Index (SSCI)-listed journals over the period 2009–13.

Tables like this are seen as important by university managers, by would-be research students, by academics looking for jobs and sometimes by potential funders, including governments. They appear to give a much neater and more detailed picture than the old, "gentlemanly" system of reputations, where Professor P would confidently pronounce that Department X was "jolly good", whereas Department Y was "a bit weak".

Table 4.1   Ranking of top PM departments by numbers of articles published in SSCI-listed journals over the period 2009–2013

Rank	Name	Number of published articles
1	University of Georgia	123
2	Cardiff University	117
3	London School of Economics	107
4	University of Manchester	98
5	Erasmus University Rotterdam	96
6	Indiana University	92
7	University of Birmingham	84
8	Australian National University	82
9	City University of Hong Kong	78
10	University of Utrecht	75

Source: Selected and adapted from Van de Walle and Van Delft (2015, table 3, p. 99).

This may be seen as progress – indeed, it very probably *is* progress, of a sort – but it is progress which simultaneously brings new problems of interpretation and potential distortion. Such figures can be genuinely informative, but only if close attention is paid to possible biases and contextual details. Unfortunately some (many?) of those who use this kind of information either cannot or will not take account of these limitations. To illustrate this, the measurement of journal publications (as in Table 4.1) has numerous snags, including the following:

1. It excludes books, yet books are still a very important component of PM. However, some other bibliometric indicators do include books (for example, Google Scholar includes citations for books, and many university systems award "points" for books as well as articles).
2. It makes no allowance for the large PM "diaspora", described above, who do not usually publish in these journals anyway, and often do not read them either. They publish, but elsewhere.
3. The results very much depend as what one classifies as "good journals", but there are some rather different ways of making this choice, which have different consequences for the results (Van de Walle and Van Delft, 2015).
4. When used to rank departments, raw journal publication scores ignore the size of the departments. Arguably, better comparisons would be obtained by dividing each departmental output by the number of academics in the department – but often this is not done. For example – looking back at Table 4.1 – there were almost certainly more PM academics at the University of Georgia (ranked 1) than at the Australian National University (ranked 8).
5. Just counting journal articles tells you nothing about the impact each article may have. One article may become a classic, cited thousands of times and influencing a whole generation, while another may receive no citations at all. There are ways of allowing for this – various ways of measuring impact factors – but these are not by any means always used when individuals and/or departments are ranked.
6. University departments can change quite quickly, whereas performance tables usually refer to papers published a few years ago, and probably first written a year or two before that. When one or two key, high-publishing individuals move from one university to another – or retire – it can have a big impact on that university's standing. This is especially true for smaller departments and those further down the list of rankings.

7. Finally, "Performance measurement and ranking is [*sic.*] by definition conservative and has homogenising tendencies. This means that once a set of indicators exists, actors will tend to adapt their behavior to make it conform to the indicators. As a result, existing diversity in the field may be crowded out" (Van de Walle and Van Delft, 2015, p. 103). Interestingly, this does not necessarily mean that those who publish more (and therefore score highly) are the true believers in these measurement systems. Recent research in Australia, New Zealand and the UK found that levels of individual research outputs were not related to the degree to which those individuals liked or disliked the measurement regimes within which they worked (Lewis, 2014).

The trend towards greater formal measurement of research outputs has now expanded to include "external" outputs – texts or other creations which have an influence on non-academic organizations or actors outside the academic world. These could include, inter alia, governments, media organizations, business corporations, trade unions or civil society organizations. Such external influences are frequently discussed under the labels of social, political and economic *relevance* – and the audit of these impacts has become an important part of national assessment exercises such as the UK's Research Excellence Framework (REF). Unsurprisingly, the measurement of "relevance" throws up as many if not more problems than the measurement of academic publications themselves. A clear and cogent analysis of these issues can be found in Bastow et al.'s *The Impact of the Social Sciences: How Academics and their Research Make a Difference* (2014).

4.4 Engagement with the world of practice

There is a long-standing relationship between PM as an academic field of study and PM as a set of practices. How does this relationship look from the academic side? How do academics get involved? This issue will be dealt with in depth later, but a brief hors d'oeuvres will be offered here, concentrating on the practical modes of involvement rather than the intellectual substance, or the ethics, of involvement. Those meatier topics will be taken up in Chapter 5.

The first point is that involvement in practice is, so to say, the iceberg of academic life. Its total volume is huge, but much of the activity is not normally visible. In all the countries where I have worked – Belgium, the Netherlands, the UK and the USA – most of my colleagues have had some form of engagement, pro bono publico. Unfortunately, I know of no systematic survey of the extent of this activity – most of it remains submerged. The current fashion, in several countries, for "social relevance" or "impact" as one measure of academic achievement may produce a better record of this activity than we have had hitherto, but the general analysis of this emerging data has yet to be written.

Perhaps the most obvious thing that academics can do is to write in practitioner publications rather than purely academic ones. This they do regularly: blogs, columns in newspapers and professional practitioner journals, reports by think tanks such as the Brookings Institution in Washington or the Institute for Public Policy Research (IPPR) in London. In the liberal democracies of western Europe and North America there are many such outlets, though there are probably fewer in some other types of regime. A few professors even graduate to the dizzy heights of TV appearances, though often they are not called in until something has gone badly wrong with the normal processes of administration (public servants are on strike, computer systems have collapsed, senior officials have become embroiled in scandal).

Academics are frequently used by public authorities to give advice (though that advice is often not taken!). Such calls can come in various forms, ranging from an informal request from a particular public official to a particular academic known to him or her, to a competitively organized tender by which whole teams of academics are recruited to perform specific functions. For example (somewhere near the middle of the aforesaid range) I once led a small team that was selected after a bidding competition to carry out an evaluation of a multi-million pound business process re-engineering project at a large NHS teaching hospital. On another occasion a successful bid resulted in the job of assessing the strengths and weaknesses of all the performance audits produced by the UK National Audit Office within a given year. At the European level, academics are frequently members of the consultancy teams which are routinely used by the European Commission to carry out evaluations of projects and programmes.

Defined tasks of this sort (in essence, applied research) are far from being the only way in which academics get involved with practitioners. Another very common route is for academics to seek or to be asked to perform (usually on a part-time basis) executive, quasi-judicial or operational roles in the public services themselves. Among my colleagues I have known governors of local schools, Justices of the Peace (a kind of lay judge in the English legal system), prison visitors, army and navy reservists and board members of public art galleries. Like a number of my fellows I have served as a non-executive member of a hospital board. At the national level some governments find it prudent to include leading academics in commissions and public inquiries, partly to tap their expertise and partly because they symbolize independence and neutrality.

4.5   A community in flux?

So the stereotype of an ivory-towered academic is particularly unsuitable for members of the PM community. Most of its members will, at some point, if not continuously, conduct applied research for the world of practice, or give consultancy-type advice, or write opinion pieces in blogs and newspapers, or themselves perform public sector roles on a part-time or on-secondment basis. These forms of engagement will almost certainly continue, and, indeed, may intensify in those countries where "relevance" and "service to the community" are incorporated as criteria in the assessment of the academic quality of individuals and departments.

In other respects, however, the community is likely to change quite fast over the coming decade. My crystal ball is no more reliable than anyone else's but it may be worth closing this chapter by identifying some of the probable trends.

First, the basic demographics of the PM community are altering – and quite fast. The generation who entered the profession in Europe and North America during the expansionary, "boom years" of the 1960s and early 1970s are now retired or retiring. And in some universities they are not all being replaced. In the climate of public sector austerity the retirement of the most senior and best paid staff is sometimes seen as an irresistable opportunity for the institution to make economies. A senior professor may thus be replaced by a (cheaper) junior lecturer, or not at all. At the time of writing a number of the departments which I know best are undergoing exactly this process, even where they have excellent records of academic productivity and public service.

In other parts of the world, however, cutbacks are not on the agenda. China, for example, has witnessed an explosion of Masters of Public

Administration (MPA) programmes over the past 10–15 years. India and Brazil are further examples of huge countries with rapidly growing economies and significant centres for the study of PM. What is more, these growing economies often have the traditions of an interventionist and developmental state (Cheung, 2012). This contrasts with the Anglosphere, where the dominant ideas (at least since the growth of influence of neo-liberal ideas in the 1970s and 1980s) have tended to frame the state, to use President Reagan's words, as the problem rather than the solution, and where more and more that which used to be publically provided has been privatized or contracted out.

Another demographic change was mentioned earlier. The representation of women among the academic ranks is growing and seems highly likely to grow further. It is hard to think of this as other than long overdue.

A final aspect of generational change is that those who are now mid-career or entering senior academic roles are likely, on average, to be better trained (particularly in social science methods) and more comfortable in exploiting the multiple research and teaching opportunities that the digital age has furnished (and will continue to enhance). These developments will, hopefully, lead to more "mixed methods", combined qualitative *and* quantitative research than we have had in the past.

Second, the internationalization of the PM community will progress even further. It has become common for young researchers, early in their careers, either to participate in international projects where they meet colleagues from other countries or to serve at least a tour of duty in another country. My most recent doctoral student was a Romanian man who took his first degree in Romania, his second in the USA and then his doctorate at the Public Governance Institute at Leuven, in Belgium. He then immediately moved to Paris to take up work with the OECD. These kinds of trajectories are less and less unusual, and, viewed collectively, raise the hope that national insularities will become less obvious in the PM scholarship of the near future. Established professors are also moving jobs internationally more than they used to. The Anglophones may have some comparative advantage here, because Australia, Canada, Ireland, New Zealand, the UK and the USA all have substantial English-speaking centres of academic PM. On the other hand, the majority of European PM professors (certainly the Danish, Dutch, Finnish, French, German, Norwegian and Swedish, plus most of the eastern European states) speak good English, so they too may well be able to take advantage of posts in the Anglosphere, if their interests lie in that direction. Many already enjoy visiting positions in North America or the UK. Further, almost all the top Anglophone PM/PA journals already have editorial boards with wide international membership. Sadly, what is currently the largest national PM community – the USA – may have further to go to participate in this growing internationalism than the European states. But even the relative introversion of many American academics may be beginning to weaken, and already a few Americans have been among the pioneers of international comparative scholarship (for example, Lynn, 2006; Peters, 1997).

Third, the long-standing dominance of the "Anglosphere" in academic PM will probably weaken (Pollitt, 2015b). Countries where both the economy and academic self-confidence are growing rapidly will come to feel less need to follow "western" ideas rather than their own. Theories and models which assign a more developmental and interventionist role to the state may once more attract wide scholarly interest.

Fourth, the community will undoubtedly be affected, as it has been in the past, by major developments in the external environment. What these will be is hard to say (some educated guesses are made in Chapter 6). But just as the global economic upheavals of the 1970s are commonly credited with a midwife role to the ideas and practices of NPM, so we may expect to see impacts on the agenda of the academic community coming from austerity, climate change and technological change – to mention only the most obvious sources.

We can expect, therefore, the PM academic community to be a community in flux. That is not a bad thing. We can look forward, perhaps, to a more globally networked and balanced, more highly professionally skilled, more gender and ethnically diverse community. Hopefully this might also be a community with stronger links to what I have termed the PM diaspora, and beyond, to other fields entirely. But what the members of this community will actually call themselves, collectively, is not by any means sure.

4.6   Key reading

There is not so much written about the PM academic community itself. It writes a great deal but is written about little. One fascinating exception is the review of academic public administration in Europe, *The European Group for Public Administration (1975–2010) Perspectives for the Future* (Bouckaert and Van de Donk, 2010). Another is the first 2011 issue of *Public Administration* (89(1)), which comprised a collection of essays in honour of the retiring editor, Rod Rhodes. Within that issue are papers which describe academic PM in the USA (Raadschelders) and the UK (Hood), as well as a characteristically lively autobiographical essay by Rod Rhodes himself.

5 The relationship with practice

... PA research needs to remain connected to PA practice. Most of our students will not become academics after graduation, but are the public administrators and public sector cadres of the future. Their education benefits from research that is informed by or speaks directly to public administration practices. Besides, how in the long run can we legitimize the substantial public spending that goes into academic PA if we are not able to demonstrate that our field maintains an active and productive dialogue with the world of practice? (Bovens, 2010, p.124)

Rather than synthesize and integrate, writers prefer to analyse and disaggregate, or the reverse of much of what the day-to-day work of public administration is all about. (Stillman, 2015, p. xviii)

Rationality is context-dependent, the context of rationality is power, and power blurs the dividing line between rationality and rationalization. (Flyvbjerg, 1998, p. 227)

5.1 Introduction

Academic PM has always had a close relationship with the world of practice. Some of the ways in which academics can get involved have been briefly described in Chapter 4. Here we will examine the relationship in greater depth, looking at how it may be changing, at what the substance of the academic input can be and at some of the ethical issues which may arise when academics get caught up in the hurly-burly of "real", politicized, public management.

In some ways – and this is very much a personal interpretation – the current professoriat, or a portion of it, seems to be moving away from this historically close bond with the world of practice. This is not a simple movement, and one can see counter-trends, but I would suggest that a gradual separation has been underway for perhaps 15–20 years.

One manifestation of this is a shift in the balance of research published in the leading PM journals. Fewer and fewer of these articles deal with problems of substance and more and more address issues of theory, of conceptualization and of method. So, for example, it has become rare indeed to see PM articles dealing directly with substantive issues such as poverty, justice, ill health or public infrastructure. Recently I was surprised to discover how little mainstream PM literature there was on two of the great challenges of our time – demographic change and climate change, despite the fact that these issues have major implications for public authorities at all levels (Pollitt, 2014, 2015a – see also Chapter 6). By contrast, there have been countless publications on theoretical and conceptual approaches to governance, innovation, transparency, leadership and public-private partnerships. When I began my career it was not at all unusual to have academic journals containing papers on how to improve public expenditure planning or civil service training or public sector organizational structures. These topics are still "live", but now they are more likely to receive coverage in consultancy reports or think tank pamphlets than in the main academic journals. At the same time, while there often used to be at least a smattering of senior practitioners attending the big academic PM conferences, such presence is nowadays increasingly rare. A degree of separation, or perhaps it is specialization, has taken place. This is not only my opinion – a number of leading scholars have noted the same trend – on both sides of the Atlantic (for example, Del Rosso, 2015; Raadschelders and Lee, 2011; Radin, 2013; Yang, 2015).

This tendency for the academic ivory tower to stand further and further away from the "action" should not be exaggerated. In PM it has not gone as far as in some other social science subjects, such as political science (Flinders, 2013). Some aspects of the relationship with practitioners actually seem to be getting closer – albeit at different rates in different countries and institutions. As mentioned in Chapter 4, in some countries criteria such as political, social and economic relevance are beginning to feature in the official assessments of research excellence (for example, in the UK Research Excellence Framework of 2014). Also, professorial chairs are now sometimes offered to individuals whose record of strictly scientific publications would not hitherto have put them in the professorial category, but who can bring in large consultancy contracts or government grants. Structurally, some leading academic centres depend heavily on this source of income. And in many countries – including the UK, the USA, Canada and the Netherlands – PM students nowadays frequently look for first choice employment with consultancy firms rather than public authorities. The consultancies seem to pay better and to offer what, superficially at least, sound like more exciting assignments. The world of practice has also crept into that inner sanctum of academia, doctoral research. Considerable numbers of doctoral candidates are nowadays supported by monies from contracted research projects whose *raison d'être* is to provide public authorities with advice on specified issues. In the UK doctoral students are now supposed to acquire "skills" and to document their "personal and professional development" and this is written into university handbooks and advice from funding and regulatory agencies. All this would suggest that the academic authorities – or at least some of them – now regard advice work as a valuable and central part of the life of an academic researcher.

Nevertheless, the trend towards "pure" research is there, and I have seen it creep over at least three departments, in the three different European countries where I have worked since 1990. What is happening in some universities is a kind of informal internal division of labour, with some staff doing the "pure" stuff and others undertaking "applied", "socially relevant" activities. This is no bad thing in itself, but can become a problem if each group looks down on the other, or if most of the academic rewards seem to go to one group and not the other.

It would seem important to understand why this polarization has been happening. Chapter 4 already offered some clues. The academic community is more measured and rated than ever before, and research money and staff have followed these ratings. The measures used to produce the ratings have tended to give greatest weight to publications in refereed journals, sometimes to a subset of these journals classified as "top" or "A". Often weight has also been given to the extent to which university units and departments attract external research funding, and the "game" of competing for such funding has itself been played out to increasingly high technical standards. Most of the brightest and the best young academics want to work in "top departments". This can be seen as partly admirable (to work alongside the best; to contribute to the highest quality, most ambitious teams) and partly self-interested (in most top departments the teaching loads are lower than elsewhere, and the flow of research funds – and sometimes the salaries themselves – are higher). However, one consequence of this trajectory is that, just as hanging onto research time has become all important for the individual, the research itself has often become more "professional", technical and "pure". It has quietly shifted further away from immediate practitioner concerns, and certainly further away from the kind of language and terminology which practitioners find it easy to understand and digest.

The argument here is not that this is all bad. It is important not to become an "either-or-ist" about these cleavages within the field of PM, or within the social sciences more generally. It is not a question of saying that this kind of work is useless and that kind always valuable. It is certainly not to claim that everyone is doing or should do the same kind of work. Rather it is a question of status and balance. The danger is that high status will be awarded to only one type of work and that that, in turn, will determine "the distribution of jobs, prizes, journal editorships and research monies" (Flinders, 2013, p. 627). Within PM, if the tendency towards separation continues, the impact could be (depending upon which faction were to become dominant) the large-scale loss of practical relevance. In my view neither this nor its opposite (the glorification of practical "relevance") would be healthy. Just as I would not want pure theorists or methods gurus to rule the PM community, neither would I want applied work with practitioners (which is often quite mundane) to receive all our academic honours and resources.

5.2   Why do practitioners want academic advice?

We have yet to establish what value academic research *could* have for the practitioner world. Let us begin by examining what might be termed the naive model. It goes something like this: in the simplest case the practitioner does not know – let us say – how to change a lightbulb. The academic has spent many years studying lightbulb-changing and comes and fixes the practitioner's problem. In the real worlds of public policy and management such simple transactions do occasionally occur, but they are unrepresentative of academic advice-giving as a whole, and are not the most *academically* significant forms of advice work. So what is wrong with this simple model of the academic as a straightforward problem-fixer? The model is misleading in at least two ways:

- Fixing specific problems is only one of the challenges faced by politicians and public servants – and it is by no means obvious that when they have problems to fix, academia is the first place they would look for a fixer.

- Problem-fixing knowledge is only one type of knowledge: academics have many other kinds, both explicit and tacit.

We take each of these points in turn.

Politicians and public servants do not exist simply to fix problems. They spend a great deal of their time maintaining relationships, defending organizational territories, trying to influence agendas and even trying to clarify their own minds on issues they have become aware of but have not yet "framed" or fixed into a slot alongside all their other policies and priorities. They search for popular issues, symbolic issues or newly emerging problems or they simply strive for greater coherence between the different issues they are called upon to address.

Thus politicians may simply want what in boxing is called a "sparring partner" – someone to try out ideas on in a safe, confidential setting. In such circumstances trust is fundamental, and politicians not infrequently choose individual academics they already know. Also, in some political cultures (for example, Switzerland, the Netherlands) politicians of different persuasions may sometimes want to use academics as neutral moderators of multi-party discussions. Academics have also sometimes been used in this role in EU meetings. This is almost the opposite of the sparring partner, because it is a calming rather than a provoking role, but deep knowledge of the specific issues is vital for both kinds of facilitation.

These kinds of motives have more to do with clarification, interpretation and definition than with providing new information or research. Structuring ideas and facilitating debate are things one would hope academics were especially well practiced at. However, that is far from being all that PM scholars can contribute. In the next section we examine some specific types of knowledge which academics can bring to the practitioners' table.

5.3 So what kinds of knowledge can academics offer that might be useful to practitioners?

Taking into account the variety of practitioners' needs and motives, one may distinguish a number of different ways in which academics are able to offer something of value to practitioners:

1. Agenda setting and re-framing: academics may be asked to identify future ("coming") issues or to reflect in challenging and innovative ways on existing problems (re-framing). This can be done through a wide variety of instruments – from the advisory commissions which are so common in Sweden and the Netherlands to dinner with the minister or a senior official. In the UK academics may be called as witnesses before Parliamentary select committees.

2. Expert moderation of inter-party or inter-institutional discussion: academics can act as the neutral but expert steering persons when there is a need to restrain factionalism or inter-institutional rivalry in policy discussions. This role is probably more common in multi-party systems than one-party governments. It also occurs in international settings.

3. Conceptual clarification: for example, what is meant by "public accountability"? How do you define "quality"? These are issues where the academic is probably familiar with a wide range of literature in which such issues are discussed, which will not be known to the average practitioner. Academics are trained to be aware of definitional issues, and can frequently help managers to sharpen their formulations. In particular academics can usefully insist that the problem(s) to be solved are defined as clearly as possible. This can help managers to work hard on problem identification and diagnosis *before* they reach for a solution. It is the opposite of bad consultancy, which has sometimes been characterized as "solutions in search of problems" (see Argyris, 2000; Jackson, 2001; Pollitt, 2003, chapter 7).

4. Questioning false assumptions: this is a kind of therapy function. Academics are trained to ferret out underlying assumptions and drag them into the light. They can do this for politicians and managers just as they can for students. This can prove surprisingly useful. For example, when discussing the modification of a public service better to fit the expressed wishes of users, it can be valuable to ask whether the reform is being carried out on the assumption that the modified service will still attract the same group of users? How reliable is this assumption? Are there trends which are changing the mix of users (for example, more very elderly users, more users who do not have good language skills, more users from a particular ethnic group?). Another example would be the assumption that bonus pay will incentivize public servants to work harder. In some circumstances this may work, but in many it apparently does not. The assumptions

about the beneficial effects of merit pay also tend to overlook the motivational impacts such systems have on those staff who do not receive a bonus.

5. Guidance on how to structure decisions: some academics are experts in decision analysis, and can advise managers on how to structure decision-making processes so as to more accurately and reliably reflect the underlying probabilities and values involved in a particular decision or series of decisions. Typically this might involve modelling the decision, making value judgements more explicit, seeking the best possible information on the probabilities of alternative outcomes and advising on how, technically, to weight probabilities with values/utilities and to discount for effects which take place at different times in the future. Decision analysis has made considerable contributions to particular parts of the public sector (for example, healthcare, environmental safety issues) but much less so to some others (for example, social work or management reform itself).

6. Advising on how best to collect data: academics usually have a strong training in social science methods. When a manager needs to know something, and that something requires research in order to find it out, she or he will frequently benefit from discussing with academics the selection of methods for data collection. It may be an issue of statistical sampling, or one of how to minimize bias in interviews, or what combination of methods to use when trying to establish what citizens want and expect from a particular service. Sometimes, of course, the academic advisers are themselves contracted to collect the data.

7. Substantive advice based on middle-range, contextually based generalizations: for example, that measuring the performance of professionally delivered human services tends to be more complex and subtle than measuring the performance of standardized administrative routines such as issuing licences or checking applications for a social security benefit (see Chapter 2, Table 2.1). Therefore it would be wise to use performance indicators in a more diagnostic, less mechanical way in healthcare and education than in more standardized "production" services (Wilson, 1989). Or (to take another example) that contracting out has worked well for certain types of service in some countries, but has proved much more controversial and difficult for other kinds of service. This kind of advice is therefore based on substantive knowledge of what is happening in a variety of settings, and in the past. Crucial to the quality of this advice, however, is a careful

discussion of the degree to which the different settings really are comparable – a discussion in which the manager receiving the advice would be well advised to take an active part. For example, telling the manager of a hospital in Birmingham how Total Quality Management (TQM) was successfully installed in a Toyota plant in Japan may be of limited use (there are too many differences in context). But telling the Birmingham manager how TQM was successfully implemented in a hospital in Manchester may be more useful/transferable.

8. Technical tips based on previous experience in other, similar contexts: for example, when measuring the time taken to deliver money benefits to claimants, set the target in terms of the average time taken to complete all payments rather than the percentage of payments made within a certain time period. The former system (averaging) will oblige staff to pay attention to *all* claims, whereas the latter (completing 90 or 95 per cent of payments within X days) may tempt staff to neglect the small percentage of really complex and difficult claims. Again, this is substantive, expert knowledge which comes from prolonged and focused exposure to empirical study. And, again, care is needed that lessons are being transferred across comparable contexts. Academics may now be gaining a relative advantage with this kind of advice. This is because rapid and repeated reorganizations undermine the institutional memory of some public sector organizations, so that they are more and more obliged to turn to outsiders for knowledge of the past – even the past histories of their own organizations and programmes (Pollitt, 2008).

Note that of these eight kinds of advice, only the last two are usually to do with directly solving problems by the application of new knowledge. Furthermore, even these two are extensively context-dependent. So these are not "eight steps to success", applicable to all tasks and times and places.

This list, though not complete, gives some idea of the variety of useful roles which PM academics can play in the world of practice. Sadly, not all practitioners realize that this range of support is on offer, and not all academics realize (or are willing to consider) how their skills could help practitioners. Much misunderstanding and unhelpful stereotyping of each camp by the other continues to take place. There is not yet widespread understanding that both learning to use advice and learning to give it require a certain amount of practice – and a good measure of mutual trust. Meeting demanding and urgent questions from powerful officials – and occasionally politicians – often turns out to be every bit as conceptually and pedagogically challenging as doing "pure" academic research. If a comprehensive history of academic PM were ever to be written it would have to give a good deal of space to the ways in which academics themselves have been stimulated by doing consultancy (see Sahlin-Andersson and Engwall, 2002; Saint-Martin, 2000). Not every step forward in theory or technique comes from the quiet contemplation of existing scientific publications, or from meticulous fieldwork, financed by "pure" academic funding. On the contrary, quite frequently advances come from academics being exposed to something unusual or unexpected while conducting advice/consultancy projects of one kind or another. In addition (although, as far as I know, this is not measured in any way) casual observation suggests that a good deal of our teaching draws on advice work. One message from this chapter is therefore that academics should talk about this more among themselves, and acknowledge that it is an important and creative part of academic lives.

5.4 Rules of engagement for PM academics working with practitioners

There are two rather different roles built into the various forms of advice-giving. One (which has a high salience for activities 1 to 4) involves challenging, re-conceptualizing and generally thinking innovatively about practitioner agendas. The other (especially activities 6 to 8, with 5 as a hybrid) is the more traditional role of the "expert" offering advice on how to do things. In this second role academics are perhaps closer to normal consultancy, whereas in the first they are confidantes and/or court jesters for those in power. The performance of both roles – especially the first – is affected by the local culture and institutional structures. So, for example, academics playing the challenging and reconceptualizing/court jester role had better be conscious of whether they are working in a highly adversarial two-party system like the British one, or a highly consensual multi-party system like the Danish one. The rules of conduct are likely to be different.

Therefore it would appear that not one set of rules of engagement is necessary, but several. That is because academics are providing not one kind of service, but a variety, and the conditions for optimizing the quality of these services also vary. For example, when acting as a vigorous sparring partner, questioning a politician's or mandarin's assumptions or deconstructing their policy concepts, the conversation requires protection and confidentiality. If the practitioner thinks his or her sparring partner will deal them a damaging blow in public, or will talk afterwards, they will not take the risk of training with the academic in the first place. On the other hand, advice on how to collect data or how to structure a decision is a much more technical task, where transparency and open dialogue are much to be desired. The key, perhaps, is to define what sort of advice it is that is wanted, to do so early and to make sure that the ground rules are both appropriate to that type (1 to 8 above) and are clearly understood by all parties concerned. Some of the disappointments which rather frequently occur (on both sides) are almost certainly due to misplaced expectations about what kind of advice is supposed to be being provided (what the Commission on the Social Sciences, 2003, jargonized as "interface management"). Academics can be rather naive about what practitioners need (and about the constraints under which they operate), while practitioners can be hideously misguided about the nature of social science knowledge and the forms in which it can be expressed. Ideally there needs to be space and time for all parties to practice the relationship – but in the hurly-burly of the political/practitioner world that is not always possible.

We may also reconsider the vexed issue of politicians "using" academics to bolster their legitimacy. A common academic reaction is that this is a terrible state of affairs, to be avoided at all costs. Certainly, when dealing with the politically and administratively powerful, we gentle academics would do well to heed the old proverb, cited by (inter alia) Chaucer, Erasmus and Shakespeare, that if we sup with the devil, we should use a long spoon. But surely that cannot mean that we should always refuse to engage in advice where a policy is already decided upon, and political positions have been taken? Academics can still make several types of contributions at that stage. They can advise on how best to collect monitoring data, they can offer substantive advice on implementation and they can sometimes give technical tips about how to solve some specific administrative problem. In short – always assuming they do not find the basic objectives of the policy repugnant or its modalities stupid – there are many ways in which academics can try to ensure that what is done is more conceptually coherent and technically efficient than it might otherwise be. None of these roles need necessarily conflict with the basic ethical principle, set out by the Dutch National Council on Research Integrity that:

The structure of the research shall not be geared towards producing the desired outcome for the client. (Royal Netherlands Academy of Arts and Sciences, 2005)

Notice that this is a principle intended to apply to the undertaking of research for practitioners – you must not skew your results to please the minister, the Academy is saying. But this admonition does not apply so directly to, say, the sparring partner role, where the academic is not actually undertaking research, but rather seeking to refresh a debate. In sum, there need not be a conflict here, but there might be. In such circumstances we academics need a long spoon and clear vision. We do not need a starry-eyed sense of our own importance because we have been asked to contribute to "policy".

If, however, the academic does find the announced policy repugnant or stupid, then his or her role should presumably shift to that of public critic rather than adviser. To become a confidential adviser in such circumstances is to enter a trap. As academics, rather than commercial consultants, our prime duty is that of "speaking truth to power" (Wildavsky, 1979). If practitioners do not wish to listen to us inside their house, we can usually choose to make ourselves heard outside. That is a great privilege, and sometimes we should use it.

Of course, it is not always easy to draw these lines. Some university units and centres have become very heavily dependent on consultancy income. They may want to speak truth to power, but they must also earn a living. All the more reason, one might think, why academics should discuss advice-giving more often, and try to develop robust, shared and public rules of engagement to cover the different types of advice-giving. It was a sign of the times that the Royal Netherlands Academy of Arts and Sciences should have felt it necessary to publish a "Declaration of Scientific Independence" (Royal Netherlands Academy of Arts and Sciences, 2005). They put the issue directly:

Researchers who perform contract research for government bodies, companies or civil organizations should be obliged, along with their clients, to state their commitment to a Declaration of Scientific Independence.

In many ways this is an admirable document, specifying principles governing publication rights, transparency of financing and so on. One small criticism might be that although a single short Declaration obviously has an attraction as a rallying point, it may not take full account of the sheer variety of relationships discussed earlier in this section.

A final comment would be that a degree of ethical purity is not necessarily bad business. It would certainly be misleading to characterize all academic consultants as high-minded and cautious, while branding all commercial consultants as rampant profit maximizers. Consider the following remark from one of the best-known books about commercial consulting:

> We should say no to projects as often as we say yes. There are many reasons to back away from business. (Block, 1999, p. 324)

5.5 Final observations

My central theme has been an argument for balance. The academic PM community should engage with the practitioner world frequently, and in a variety of ways. At the same time, however, it should seek to define the terms of those various forms of engagement. Clear models are needed, and more open collective discussion within the academic community than has usually been in evidence in the past. The community needs to remain on guard about the real possibilities of the distortion or concealment of research evidence and the incorporation of nominally independent academics to larger organizational and political purposes. Within university departments and units relationships need to be constantly monitored and managed to try to ensure that neither the "pure" nor the "applied" tribes of PM academics totally dominate the other. All this is much easier said than done. The lure of consultancy money, the proximity to powerful politicians and officials and the dazzle of possible media prominence can all appear irresistible to the modestly paid lecturer with a heavy teaching load (not to speak of the empire-building dean or vice-chancellor). The life of a would-be "pracademic" is not an easy one. The balancing act is one where a faltering of attention can easily lead to a fall. Yet, at the same time, like other high wire occupations, it can be exciting and – for a period anyway – totally absorbing.

6 Current and future issues ("megatrends")

Only a higher productivity route can offer public sector workers the opportunities to be better paid, to work in a clearly modern and efficient workplace, and to deliver services in a fashion that commands societal respect. The onset of austerity after 2008 greatly strengthened these imperatives. (Dunleavy and Carrera, 2013, p. 322)

There has been no parallel issue to that of humanly induced climate change for any previous civilization. No previous society has intervened in nature even remotely to the degree to which we do on an everyday basis. (Giddens, 2015, p. 157)

6.1 Introduction

We have looked at theories, at methods and at the PM academic community. We have not yet said very much about the actual public sector problems or issues this community is looking at or surrounded by (these two things are by no means necessarily the same!). In this chapter we will try to do that.

The chapter will not be confined to those topics which are currently attracting most interest in PM journals. That is a legitimate though somewhat introverted way of examining what issues face the community. So from Section 6.3 onwards I will take a more extrovert approach, looking at the wider world and asking what issues "out there" are likely to have major impacts on PM over the next decade or more. The rise of NPM was of this kind – it was happening in the practitioner world for some years before PM academics began to conceptualize it, label it and theorize about its nature and consequences. One of its principal causes appears to have been the global economic shocks of the 1970s, and their impacts on public finances. Such external forces, impacting on many public sectors simultaneously and over prolonged periods of time, are sometimes referred to as "megatrends" (KPMG, 2013a).

6.2 What are academics currently focusing on?

First, however, we will look at the PM journals and see what topics appear to be growing in popularity and prominence. Of course this is far from reliable as a prediction of what will actually be important in five or ten years time. Current trends can be rapidly upset in at least two ways. First, new ideas can arise within the PM academic community itself, and can push their way to the front. After all, academic careers are sometimes built on proclaiming new ideas (or sometimes old ideas dressed up in new terminology!). This can happen quite fast, so there can be no guarantee that today's "top ten" will still be high in the charts in five years time. Second, as indicated earlier, external events can make such an impact that PM scholars are obliged to pay them some attention.

Among those topics which have grown in academic salience over the past decade are the following:

- trust
- transparency
- innovation
- governance (both nationally and internationally)
- networks and partnerships
- e-government/digitalization
- performance management
- public service motivation
- leadership
- co-production
- crisis management (including the management of both "natural" disasters – such as floods or earthquakes – and man-made disasters, such as terrorist attacks).

It should immediately be confessed that this list has been arrived at in a fairly impressionistic manner. I have simply taken some of the mainline journals from both sides of the Atlantic (*International Review of Administrative Sciences, Public Administration, Public Administration Review, Public Management Review, Public Money and Management*) from my shelves and looked back through their lists of contents for the past five years. All the above items stand out as featuring in a large number of titles and abstracts. To do this kind of analysis more rigorously would require a great deal of time and thought (see Raadschelders and Lee, 2011, pp. 20–22). Inter alia one would have to deal with problems such as articles which cover combinations of these topics, changes in categories and labels over time, and changes in the total number (volume) of articles published. However, this list will have to serve for present purposes. All these topics have not simply generated streams of articles, they have also been used as themes for many conferences and journal special issues.

Some of these topics are closely inter-related. For example, greater transparency in public agencies is supposed to increase trust, and higher trust improves the workings of networks and partnerships. Networks are one of the principal modalities of governance ("networked governance"). Or again, strong leadership is said to be an essential ingredient in large-scale e-government projects, which can otherwise easily begin to drift in time, money and focus. Leadership is also frequently seen as a key factor in crisis management. There is therefore a degree of connection between some of these "headline" issues.

All these topics can be addressed at the local level, national level or on a high plane of abstraction. One can examine in quite detailed and practical terms how a particular agency in a particular country encourages innovation, or one can compare rates of public sector innovation across whole governments, or one can attempt to build a general model of innovation, constructed of those elements which evidence indicates are necessary or sufficient for encouraging public sector staff to take the risks of innovating.

Notice that all these topics can be considered as solutions to one or more real-world problems. They *can* be discussed and presented in a very abstract way – playing with alternative definitions and abstract models, but they all also have some (real or alleged) value in solving perceived contemporary problems. Thus increasing innovation, for example, is supposed to enable the public sector to adapt to fiscal austerity while retaining high quality services. Leadership is held to be essential in achieving all sorts of desirable goals, ranging from high staff motivation, through high performance to clearer accountability. Governance, networking and partnerships are regularly proposed as a way forward (if not *the* way forward) in a context where the formal hierarchical authority of governments is said to have dwindled. Governments, it is said, must now govern by working through partnerships with private sector corporations and civil society associations. Co-production (the engagement of citizens in the design, delivery and evaluation of public services) is claimed to increase public trust and stimulate innovation

(Alford and O'Flynn, 2012). Crisis management is obviously a sub-field which hopes to find better ways of planning for and responding to events when disaster strikes. All this is yet further evidence of the close links between the academic community and the world of practice.

As important as what is on this list is what is not. Some of the classic topics of academic PM in the 1960s and 1970s have faded. In the 2010s we see fewer articles analysing the bureaucratic machinery of central or local governments. There are also fewer pieces on the recruitment and training of civil servants, and on formal accountability mechanisms such as legislative committees or national audit offices. Major national reform programmes attract some attention, but seemingly less than they used to. These topics have by no means completely disappeared, but they are not as "hot" as they used to be. Although real-world problems still clearly influence academic agendas, nowadays the academic response tends to be more highly conceptualized and theorized. Issues are more often rendered into a more abstract academic form – the difficulties the Ministry of X is having persuading local authorities and pressure groups of its views on problem Y will be conceptualized and presented as a case of "multi-level governance". There are fewer straight commentaries or descriptive analytic or historical narrative pieces than there used to be.

A different approach to identifying current and future topics is taken in a recent American survey of the field, *Public Administration Evolving: From Foundations to the Future* (Guy and Rubin, 2015). In this collection most of the chapters are framed as movements, from something in the past to something in the future. Their selection (self-admittedly US-centric) is as follows:

1. From inter-governmental to inter-sectoral. This means that the (US) focus used to be on relations between different (vertical) levels of government, but is increasingly on more horizontal relations between governments, non-profit and private sector for-profit partnerships and networks. This does not mean that the old problems of vertical structures have gone away – they are still there but are now interwoven with even more complex horizontal relations.

2. From trust to doubt. As public trust in politicians and governments has fallen, so many if not most government actions become more problematic, as the authorities can no longer rely on public confidence and acquiescence. There is

a need to reform US politics, which has recently become too ideologically divisive and driven by self-interest. (Readers should note here that the USA has tended to have low levels of trust in government compared with many European states, such as France, Germany, the Netherlands and the Nordics.)

3. From local to global. The globalization of finance, economic activity and rapid communications has been accompanied by a growth in the need for and awareness of "good governance". Good governance, whether nationally or internationally, requires governments to have the capacity to coordinate policies with other governments, deliver services (often through non-governmental partners) and establish procedures for ensuring both performance and accountability.

4. From silos to networks: hierarchy and heterarchy. This theme also picks up on the vertical/horizontal distinction. The argument is that collaboration within networks has become vastly more important, and that it demands a different set of skills from managing within traditional hierarchical bureaucracies. Networking in itself is no panacea: collaborations often fail or involve controversies and inefficiencies. It can be done well or badly, and by no means suits every problem or situation.

5. From administration to management. (The PM/PA distinction was addressed in Chapter 1, Section 1.3.) Yang (2015) comes to the conclusions that "management has always been part of public administration", and that "a scientific agenda on management should not be used as an excuse to exclude normative theories, value-laden topics, alternative research methods, or interaction with practitioners" (p. 118).

6. From outputs to outcomes. Here the idea is that performance management should not remain content with focusing on what the public organization produces (outputs) but on what final impacts these have on the outside world (social and economic outcomes). It is acknowledged, however, that this ambition has been pursued for many years, with only mixed results. Many obstacles to getting a clear picture of causes and outcomes need to be recognized and addressed. A further comment would be that the need to give outcomes at least equal treatment with outputs has been widely proposed in the academic literature for at least a quarter of a century.

7. From paper to cloud. There is a widespread expectation that changes in IT will continue to have major impacts on PM. Foreseen developments include probability analysis and big data

analytics (see, for example, Mayer-Schönberger and Cukier, 2013) together with privacy and security issues. There are particular concerns about the degree to which governments are already becoming dependent on cloud computing which is supplied and controlled by external, private corporations, and also the extent to which public authorities can retain sufficient in-house IT expertise to understand their own needs and the relative advantages and disadvantages of different proffered "solutions". (Technological change is dealt with in Section 6.5.)

8. From sameness to differentness. This charts the gradual, halting movement away from a public sector workplace dominated by white males, and the struggle against discrimination on the basis of race, ethnicity, colour, nationality, age or disability – plus, more recently, sexual or gender identity. The argument is that the very concept of "differentness" has changed and expanded, and that there is much work still to be done – for example, in respect of family responsibilities discrimination (FRD). This part of the discussion is particularly Americo-centric. Yet at the same time, although the framework of law and institutions is different elsewhere, many of these types of discrimination *are* present in many other countries – in Asia, Africa, Europe and South America. To take just one example, increased migration both within the EU and into the EU makes the representativeness of the staff of many kinds of public agency in EU member states a more salient issue.

9. From equality to social equity. This story reflects a movement from a concentration on equal rights for all citizens to a wider concern that everyone should be fairly treated – including minorities. Public services should be equally available to all races/ethnicities, genders, income levels, ability levels and sexual orientations, *in practice*. This notion of social equity has gradually found its place in public sector codes of ethics and practice, but its application continues to throw up new challenges – for example, in respect of internet-based services.

10. From ethical expectations to professional standards. Here there has been a movement from a position where careful recruitment was supposed to result in staff who would naturally behave in ethical ways (because they were "public spirited") to a more formalized system. In the latter increasingly elaborate attempts have been made to write down and codify what is expected of public servants as sets of professional standards. What is more, the scope of these standards has broadened to include new, or newly recognized issues.

It is obvious that some of these (especially 2, 3, 4, 6 and 7) echo my earlier list of popular journal topics. Some, however, are not so well covered by the mainstream PM journals – 8 and 9, for example. It is also clear that most of the list of issues affect many more countries than just the USA. It would be fascinating to compare this US list with listings from other countries, but unfortunately that is not yet possible. One might speculate, for instance, that in quite a few countries official corruption, both "grand" and petty, would feature in the list. To give you some idea of the scale of this problem, it has been calculated that if all EU states were to control corruption as well as Denmark has done, they would in one year collect additional taxes worth twice the EU budget, effectively ending the current crisis over fiscal imbalances in the eurozone (Mungiu-Pippidi, 2015). Globally, when 114 000 respondents in 107 countries were surveyed in 2013, 27 per cent reported having paid a bribe during the previous 12 months. China, for example, is well known to have extensive corruption problems, and its current government has declared itself bent on rooting it out and punishing the officials involved. In many countries discrimination in both public sector appointments and the availability of public services or government contracts is based on, say, tribalism or religion or political party membership. Such forms of discrimination are also aspects of corruption. We can be confident that these issues will not suddenly evaporate, but will be the sites for many future struggles.

6.3   External "megatrends"

The medium term future public sectors are likely to be shaped by major external forces, just as the public sectors of the past have been (Andrews, 2013; Lynn, 2006; Pollitt and Bouckaert, 2009). Two brief historical examples will illustrate the point. First, there were the effects of the global economic turmoil of the 1970s as midwife to widespread public sector reform programmes across Europe and beyond, and to the birth of NPM. Subsequently this generated a huge academic industry (see, for example, Dunleavy et al., 2006a; Hood and Dixon, 2015; Hood and Peters, 2004). Second, there have been the large changes in the organization of public agencies which have resulted from their progressive digitalization since the early 1980s. These too have resulted in a new province of academic PM, in the shape of e-government studies (for example, Bekkers and Homburg, 2005; Dunleavy et al., 2006b; Lee and Reed, 2015; Pollitt, 2012; Snellen and Van de Donk, 1998).

Such external forces may be economic, technological, political or cultural, but they oblige public administrations to change their skills, their attitudes, their practices and their organizations. These changes, in turn, almost inevitably attract academic attention, not to speak of research grants and consultancy.

Such outside forces are not the only factor in play. They act upon and through a set of existing institutional structures, cultures and processes, and this set varies considerably from one country to another. For example, in some countries the academic PM community is close to government and is used to providing regular advice. In others the academics are at a greater distance or even ignored. Outside forces also act alongside and through other more endogenous influences, such as new management ideas and doctrines. But they do have impacts, both on practice and on academic PM. The question of what such external trends are likely to be is therefore an important one.

Some external trends are very clear and highly probable. In the immediate future we can be confident that fiscal stress will continue to dominate the agendas in most EU member states and in North America (Kickert and Randma-Liiv, 2015). Austerity is not going to go away soon. Although triggered by the global financial crisis and the ensuing economic and eurozone crises, fiscal restraint in the public sector is also a result of underlying demographic, social and technological trends which will continue to lead to historically high levels of demand for public services and benefits. To put it bluntly, we will have more people living longer and – thanks to technology – more we can do for them, but we will not be able to afford to actually do all these things. Therefore painful choices will have to be made, and painful priorities either agreed or imposed.

A second trend is technological change. The public sector has already been significantly affected by technological change – most obviously, but by no means only, by digitalization and the advent of the internet (Dunleavy and Carrera, 2013; Dunleavy et al., 2006b; Pollitt, 2012). We have good reasons to expect that technological change will continue. In the near future not only will more and more public services go online, but we will also be moving into an era of even higher-tech medicine, of robotics and a variety of automatic security systems and of continuing change in modes of transport and communications. Technological change links closely with the previous point: in medicine, for example, it is almost inconceivable that the gap between what can be done and what can be afforded will be eliminated. Public policymaking is bound to make a major contribution to such awkward choices, just as it has done in the past.

There are other deeply consequential trends. For example, barring global catastrophes of disease or war, we can be sure that in the near future the population of elderly people in Europe will continue to grow larger relative to that of younger people, because these soon-to-be-old people already exist. We also know that this demographic shift will considerably increase the demand for many kinds of healthcare and social care services, most of which are currently paid for and provided by – or at least extensively subsidized by – public authorities. We have known for decades that this is going to be a public sector pressure point.

Other external circumstances appear very likely but are somewhat harder to predict in any detail. For example, climate change is usually investigated by means of huge and complex computerized models. Rising sea levels and the growth of extreme weather episodes (climate change) have extensive implications for public authorities right across the globe, but while the great weight of scientific opinion predicts such changes, we are much less sure of exactly when, where and how fast these levels and episodes will increase. There are considerable scientific debates about the best methodologies for making estimates and, in any case, the rates and extent of change can be affected by public policy decisions which have yet to be taken or implemented. Nevertheless, there is an overwhelming consensus that global warming is underway, and that it lies behind a number of extreme and damaging weather episodes we have already suffered (IPCC, 2007, pp. 2–5, 2014).

All the above megatrends are having and/or will have widespread impacts on many countries. They are global in extent and consequence. That does not mean that their effects are uniform right across the globe – far from it. Fiscal austerity is present in western Europe and North America, but not in China, India or Brazil (Kickert and Randma-Liiv, 2015). Of course these latter countries are affected, in so far as the sluggish economies of the west buy fewer of their exports, and also because their investments in the west are adversely affected, but they are not engaged in radically cutting back public programmes as in, say, Ireland, the Netherlands, Portugal, Italy, the UK and the USA. Demographic change is another geographically limited problem, at least in the sense that the proportion of young people in the populations of most Southeast Asian or Latin American countries are much higher than in western Europe. Technological change at first may seem more universal – but that is something of an illusion. New technologies actually spread across the world in a very uneven fashion (Pollitt, 2012, pp. 27–8). Africa, for example, remains very short in its number of internet connections per head of population, compared to more developed parts of the world. Climate change is perhaps the most globally pervasive of our megatrends, but even here the predictions are for widely varying impacts by region. Extreme heat and drought may be suffered by North Africa and the Mediterranean countries, while Finland and Sweden actually gain a moderately longer, warmer growing season.

Other external events are much more uncertain. We know that they may come about but the "if" and "when" questions are impossible to offer any safe answer to. For example, if certain viruses improved their ability to "jump" from other species to human beings, then the world could be faced with pandemics that would involve governments in many vital ways. This chapter does not cover these (hopefully) lower probability events.

This "megatrends" way of approaching the future has both advantages and disadvantages. One advantage is that it focuses on relatively concrete external events and circumstances rather than the more abstract world of models and concepts of management. A disadvantage, however, is that it starts quite a long way from the specifics of particular organizations and their powers, personnel and budgets. Thus, what we learn may not be easily translatable into immediate prescriptions for organizational change or managerial action. Nevertheless, awareness of megatrends does at least point us towards certain PM capacities and skills that are highly likely to be needed in the near future.

6.4 Fiscal austerity

After a slow start, we are, at the time of writing, beginning to see a stream of PM articles and books on the nature and consequences of fiscal austerity (Hood et al., 2014; Kickert and Randma-Liiv, 2015). This is highly desirable, because prolonged austerity has serious implications for the future of public sectors and their staff. These include:

- Hiring freezes, which have been very common across the EU. These save money, but they also result in an ageing workforce which may possess an increasingly inappropriate set of skills.
- Redundancies. Also widespread. In Greece (the most extreme case of austerity) state employment fell by 30 per cent, and the wage bill by 35 per cent, between 2008 and 2014.
- Reductions and changes in pension entitlements for public sector staff. Again, there have been many instances, in many countries.
- Budget cuts. In the UK, for example, the 2010–15 Conservative/ Liberal Democrat coalition government imposed overall cuts of about 30 per cent on the budgets of local authorities.
- The motivational issue that the staff who are most committed to serving the public find they cannot sustain the level of service they previously provided. This provokes disillusionment and, if other opportunities present themselves, loss of some of the most committed staff.
- Recruitment problems (where there is not already a recruitment freeze) because the public service looks less attractive, and its material rewards are reduced or frozen.
- A pressing need for higher rates of innovation – in order to "do more with less".
- Popular protests (and the rise of populist political parties) arising from the perception that the state is cutting back "entitlements" – often to the most vulnerable members of the community. It could be that the general decline in "trust in government" in international surveys since 2007 has a lot to do with the austerity policies by which most governments have responded to the fiscal crisis (OECD, 2015, p. 158). These have tended to amplify income inequalities – to the point where the OECD itself has begun to headline the need for more "inclusive" and "sustainable" policies (OECD, 2015, p. 8).

Unlike, say, demographic change, austerity is a policy rather than a deeply rooted social change and, as such, could in principle be un-chosen, just it was previously chosen (Blyth, 2013). At present, however, this seems unlikely. On the contrary, most western countries are planning on further economies stretching many years ahead. In this situation most parts of the public sector experience austerity not as something optional or avoidable, but as something imposed. Schools, universities, social care departments, hospitals, police forces, fire brigades – all these and more are simply faced with cuts or freezes to their annual budgets. As one former UK local government chief executive put it:

> The agenda for the foreseeable future for senior managers is reduced budgets, staff, capacity, services and investment, and increased workload, working hours, budget consultations and stress levels. (Barrow, 2015, p. 329)

The current period of austerity is beginning to seem different from previous episodes of cutbacks not only in its breadth (so many countries) but also in its length. After five years of austerity, there is little prospect of any return to growth and expansion in most public services (Kickert and Randma-Liiv, 2015). There is no vision of a "return to normal". On the contrary, a number of leading politicians and some of the big management consultancies are envisaging a permanent reduction in the size of the public sector: a "small state" would become the "new normal" (KPMG, 2013a, 2013b). Many public services previously supplied by state agencies will be contracted out or provided within public-private partnerships. The implications of this for academic PM would be considerable: in effect, the size and importance of the main object of our academic attention would shrink.

6.5   Technological change

Technological change has already required both public officials and citizens to become at least minimally competent in handling computers and the internet. The "digital divide", experts say, should diminish as the elderly, pre-computer generation dies out, and as various parts of the world (most noticeably Africa) "catch up" with the high rate of connectivity already achieved in the affluent west.

Going online is, however, only the start of a long and complex process. Technological change has affected and will affect the public sector in a myriad of ways (Pollitt, 2012). For example:

- Changing technologies change the tasks which public officials have to carry out. Police need to learn how to track internet criminals, doctors can check body monitors on patients remotely and so on. Often new technologies also change the places in which public sector work is done. Staff no longer need to be physically close to the citizen/user/client. They may even be located in another country. At the time of writing UK and US military staff, sitting in bases in their own countries, control drones flying above Afghanistan and Iraq, which are capable, on receiving instructions, of dispatching deadly missiles at designated targets.

- Changing technologies also carry large implications for the recruitment, training and retraining of public officials. New skills are needed and the more rapidly the technological work environment evolves, the more frequently existing staff will require updating. One concern is that if governments fail to retain sufficient up-to-date expertise in-house, they will likely fail to make sensible IT purchases/investments (Dunleavy et al., 2006b).

- New technologies are often major investments for public agencies, and will therefore inevitably compete with other possible budget allocations, such as extra staff, salaries or buildings. A 2014 OECD survey of 23 countries showed 579 government IT projects with budgets of over US$10 million (OECD, 2015, p. 148).

- Changing technologies can influence the productivity of public services (Dunleavy and Carrera, 2013). Records can be retrieved, applications can be processed, fresh data can be formulated and disseminated far, far faster than ever before. For a wide range of services the costs of dealing with members of the public can be greatly reduced because handling requests and enquiries can be done far more cheaply via the internet than by having counters in office buildings to which members of the public have to come, or by using conventional post. On the other hand, many countries have witnessed expensive, large-scale attempts to install advanced public computer systems which have run far over time and over budget, and which, in the end, have not delivered the service improvements originally promised (Dunleavy and Carrera, 2013; Dunleavy et al., 2006b).

- Changing technologies can influence the scope, quality and accuracy of public services. For the police, for example, DNA testing has made a huge difference to the speed and confidence with which they can solve many crimes. Similarly, advances in technology have vastly improved both diagnosis and treatment in many areas of healthcare. Gene sequencing, for example, has already provided valuable insights to the nature of many diseases and disorders, while stem cell research promises a whole range of new curative interventions.

- Changing technologies affect how citizens interface with public services. Instead of going into a public office and talking to an official they will now more often sit at home in front of a computer screen (or use their smartphone, wherever they are) and interact with a public website. Across the OECD in 2014, 49 per cent of individuals had used the internet to get information from public authorities, and 33 per cent had filed government forms electronically (OECD, 2015, p. 152). There was also widespread government/citizen interaction on the so-called "social media". Thus far we have very little knowledge about how such "disembodied" connections may influence citizen attitudes to particular public services or even to government as whole (Pollitt, 2012, pp. 64–5).

● Changing technologies can bring to the forefront complex trade-offs between service effectiveness, state security and citizen privacy. At the time of writing this book US PM websites were full of debate about a security breach in which computer system hackers had managed to gain access to more than 21.5 million federal government individual personnel records. Similar large-scale breaches of security or losses of sensitive data have occurred in other countries. At the same time very extensive media coverage was being given to large-scale government "snooping" exercises in the USA and the UK, in which government security agencies had apparently tapped into millions of their citizens' emails and telephone calls. A further dimension to some of the privacy problems is that often the data are actually held by, or meant to be protected by, private sector companies working on government contracts, rather than by the departments or agencies themselves.

PM academics have been reasonably prolific in their writings about e-government (for example, Bekkers and Homberg, 2005; Dunleavy et al., 2006b; Lee and Reed, 2015; Pollitt, 2012; Snellen and Van de Donk, 1998). Other aspects of technological change – such as robotics, bio-technology applications or police surveillance and forensic equipment – have received much less attention. It remains to be seen when main-line PM will fully understand that the implications of technological change for the public sector go much wider and deeper than just developing online government. This broader understanding is not yet evident in the contents of the core PM journals.

6.6   Demographic change

In the EU, North America and Japan the population is getting older (Table 6.1).

Table 6.1 Ageing populations

	Population over 65 as a percentage of working age population (15–64)	
	2010 (%)	2025 (%)
France	25.9	35.8
Germany	30.9	40.7
Italy	31.1	38.8
UK	25.2	31.4

Source: Derived from KPMG (2013b).

People living longer – on average – has major implications for public authorities. In most developed countries the two largest government budget items are pensions and healthcare expenditure. Both rise as citizens live longer. But the full range of implications goes far beyond this (Harper and Hamblin, 2014). Consider the following:

- Pension systems need to be significantly adjusted (are already being adjusted) so that the pension funds – both public and private – can afford to go on paying their pensions to more recipients and over longer average periods.
- Healthcare systems need to be prepared to deal with an increased volume of ill health and disability. Many conditions (including, for instance, some cancers, arthritis, hearing loss) increase in incidence with age. The cost implications of these trends are large.
- Social care systems will also have to adjust to the increase of elderly citizens. The provision of facilities and services which will enable them to continue to participate in the community, to work, to meet others, to take exercise and to keep their skills up-to-date will require a good deal of planning and investment – partly from the private and voluntary sectors but also from public sector agencies.
- As many people live longer and retain good basic health, the conventional regulations and structures of many labour markets begin to look inappropriate. Why force people to retire when they are 60 or 65 if they can continue to work and they want to do so? Or, to put the issue another way, why throw away all that experience and skill while it can still serve society through regular

employment? This consideration applies equally to public sector and private sector employment.

- Many public service staff may need further training to improve their skills in dealing with elderly service users. It is still far too often assumed that a slow reaction from an elderly client indicates that they are confused or stupid. In fact it may well simply be that they are hard of hearing or are cognitively that little bit slower to process new information than the 20-something or 30-something staff who are dealing with them. The elderly citizen-client may be highly intelligent and equally articulate, but simply needs a little more help or time to get going.
- Last but not least, public authorities have a role to play in reshaping popular stereotypes of old age. Traditional assumptions need to be challenged and more diversified and active images of what it is to be 70 or 80 made more salient.

Mainstream PM journals have not yet carried much material on the implications of demographic change. Social policy journals have carried more and, of course, specialist demographic publications have dealt extensively with this megatrend. It could be expected that the PM scholarly community will soon become more active on this topic.

6.7   Climate change

At first sight climate change may seem at something of a distance from the day-to-day preoccupations of students of PM. In fact, however, climate change carries major implications for public authorities across many sectors and at all levels. This observation applies to both mitigation policies (designed to reduce the emission of greenhouse gases) and adaptation policies (aimed at better protecting our societies from the consequences of global warming). Again, consider the following:

- Building regulations in most parts of the world need to be changed to reflect both the priority of economizing on energy use (including better insulation) and the increased incidence of extreme weather events (storms, floods).
- Energy generation and transmission systems require reappraisal with the aim of reducing the emission of "greenhouse gases". Some governments (such as Germany's) have announced ambitious plans to move away from a dependency on fossil fuels and towards a much higher proportion of electricity generation

from sustainable sources. Other governments, however (such as Poland's), have initially moved to defend their traditional coal industry.

- Transport systems – on the ground, in the air and at sea – need to be looked at afresh with an eye to radically reducing carbon dioxide (CO_2) emissions and hydrocarbon consumption. This will entail, inter alia, new regulatory frameworks and tax instruments which apply both nationally and internationally.

- Agricultural systems in many parts of the world will undergo transitions, as the changing climate makes it more difficult to grow traditional crops (but perhaps possible to grow new crops). Patterns of plant and animal diseases and pests are already shifting. These changes will trigger corresponding changes in the pattern of agricultural regulation and subsidy. For example, the EU Common Agricultural Policy (CAP) remains the single largest budget item for the European Commission, and Commission officials are already funding studies into the impacts of global warming on agriculture in the different regions of the continent.

- The many populated areas of the world that are low-lying, and close to the sea or to large rivers, must urgently reconsider their future security. Some (but how to decide which?) will have to be abandoned – there is simply not enough money, time or resource to safeguard all the areas under threat. Some may need major new infrastructural developments better to protect them against floods. Emergency planning will probably need revision to reflect the increased frequency of major risks. Insurance arrangements will have to be changed.

- The emergency services may need new training, more equipment and staff, and new kinds of equipment to deal with the higher incidence and extent of extreme events.

- The whole process of climate change implies greatly enhanced and more sophisticated systems for monitoring weather patterns and other natural events. Again, these will need to be able to operate in a coordinated way at local, national and international levels.

- Because climate change is so pervasive and multiple in its effects there will be a pressing need for governments to plan and respond in more "horizontal" ("joined-up") ways. Operations in different sectors and at different levels will need to be coordinated if they are to have optimal impacts.

- A huge programme of public education, combined with incentives, may be needed in order to explain to citizens how their own lifestyles and practices can contribute to combating the adverse effects of climate change.

- There are considerable immigration and security concerns attaching to the consequences of climate change. For example, living conditions in parts of North Africa and southern Europe are likely to become more and more difficult, with rising temperatures, dwindling water supplies and failing crops. Related problems exist in other parts of the world (for example, large parts of Southeast Asia are vulnerable to rising sea levels). These pressures may well lead to large-scale population movements and/or to conflicts over possession of water supplies. There are even discussions of the possibility of climate change crime and terrorism (Maas et al., 2013).

- There is already and will continue to be a need for diplomatic skills and new international coordinating bodies and procedures, because no one country can successfully tackle the effects of climate change on its own. The miserable failure of the 2009 Copenhagen climate conference was an illustration of the consequences of the play of national vested interests, poor coordination and lack of political understanding of the magnitude of the issues (Klein, 2015).

Overall, therefore, the impacts of climate change on public authorities would appear to be almost endless. As one early book on the governance of climate change put it, this is "the greatest collective action problem the world currently faces" (Bulkeley and Newell, 2010, p. 111).

Neither should it be supposed that all this lies some way into the future. "Dramatic climate change transformations are creating risks, not just for our remote future but for our *immediate future*" (Giddens, 2015, p. 155, emphasis in the original; Klein, 2015). In fact climate change is also already with us. Although individual storms or floods cannot be attributed with any certainty to global warming the increased overall incidence of these things can. There have already been floods, droughts, heat waves and changes in the distributions of various pests and diseases which seem highly likely to be connected to the general trend, and which have claimed their toll in human lives and livelihoods (Pollitt, 2015a). A bestselling journalistic study offers many stark examples and concludes that "climate change puts us on such a tight and unforgiving deadline" (Klein, 2015, p. 26).

At the time of writing this book mainline PM publications had carried very few articles about climate change (Pollitt, 2015a). PM scholars have, however, made more significant contributions to multidisciplinary (non-PM) publications (for example, Termeer et al., 2011). Overall, however, the impact of climate change on PM scholarship cannot be described as large. My own view is that this state of affairs cannot possibly last much longer, and that the management and implementation of the many innovatory policies and processes that will inevitably result from climate change will lead to an upsurge of activity within the PM academic community, nationally and internationally. I may be wrong, but I find it hard to see how our community could ignore this gigantic challenge.

6.8   Interactions

The megatrends considered above are not independent. They interact in many complex ways. They do this in both positive and negative directions – altogether in far more ways than can be specified, let alone assessed, here. Just two examples will be offered, one of positive interactions and the other of negative interactions.

Technological innovation is expected to be an important part of the solutions to both demographic change and climate change. The larger elderly population, it is said, will be able to access much of the healthcare it will need remotely – fewer trips to the doctor's office will be necessary, and people with mobility problems will be able to receive more care at home. Automatic sensors on or in the body of the patient will transmit data to the doctor and will trigger warnings when particular measures (blood pressure, sugar levels and so on) reach danger levels (May et al., 2005). Remote interviews with doctors can be arranged on Skype or CCTV or in other ways. Pharmaceuticals can be ordered on the internet and delivered to the patient's home. For those who are restricted in their mobility or strength many household tasks will be performed by robots, both in homes and hospitals.

Negative interactions exist between austerity, on the one hand, and both demographic change and climate change, on the other. If we take the example given immediately above, the implementation of remote care for the elderly will require a considerable up-front investment in sensor systems, wi-fi connections and so on. In most western countries much of that investment would come from the public purse, but in many of those countries long-term investment programmes have featured among the first casualties of public sector cuts. For politicians it is often less painful to cut investment (a future benefit that citizens are not yet receiving) than to cut current expenditure programmes (where citizens/voters will immediately notice). Many OECD governments have recently done just that (OECD, 2015). This same argument applies to climate change, in the sense that both adaptation and mitigation efforts frequently point to major new investments as the first step. New forms of energy generation and transmission are often very expensive in capital terms. New flood defences and water management systems, and retro-fitting existing buildings to be more climate-resilient also require large infrastructural investments, the benefits of which may not be seen for years ahead. In her bestseller, Naomi Klein put it like this:

> There are many important debates to be had about the best way to respond to climate change . . . There is, however, no scenario in which we can avoid wartime levels of spending in the public sector – not if we are serious about preventing catastrophic levels of warming, and minimizing the destructive potential of the coming storms. (Klein, 2015, p. 108)

6.9   Concluding observations

This has been a chapter about the future. The aim has been to open out horizons and identify some (only some) of the forces that will act on public sectors over the next decade and more. It has been assumed that academic PM will recognize these pressures and devote some of its energies to studying them. Futurology is, of course, a risky business, and I may be wrong. Optimistically, however, I believe that the chances of all these suggestions being wrong are quite small. The megatrends examined above are already, tangibly, with us and it is not in their natures suddenly to cease and disappear.

At the moment there appears to be something of a disconnect between the "top ten" popular topics and themes in PM journals and the looming challenges associated with our megatrends. Articles on austerity are beginning to come through, but there is still little in mainstream PM journals on technological change, other than e-government, or on demographic change or global warming. Yet – to take an optimistic stance – this disconnect, though real enough, is not too wide or deep. A number of the themes which are already academically popular *could* be made highly relevant to the identified megatrends. Ideas of co-production, for example, could be applied to the business of domestic energy saving and a shift to sustainable sources. Theories of network management and partnership (as well as co-production) could be used in the development of ways of supporting a much larger population of the elderly. Performance management could be turned upon the matter of setting and monitoring national or local or organizational targets for reducing CO_2 emissions. And so on. The point is that these theories and concepts have the potential for application to many of the problems thrown up by the megatrends, but as yet they simply have not been much used in this way.

What is unmistakably clear is that the practitioner world of western PM is currently living through "hard times", and that this will impact on (is already impacting on) academic PM in a number of different ways. It will reduce (has already reduced) the public finance going into universities, and this puts pressure on PM teaching and research. But austerity plus technological change plus demographic change plus climate change will also face academic PM with a long agenda of new issues. One aspect of this new agenda is that much of it points to the need for a multi-disciplinary or interdisciplinary response. The study of technological change is inherently a multi-disciplinary exercise, with engineers and technologists working alongside psychologists, sociologists, economists and, hopefully, PM scholars. Working on the effects of demographic change means PM scholars cooperating closely with demographers, social and healthcare experts, housing and planning scholars and so on. Researching the impacts of climate change will need PM scholars to gain some understanding of the science of climate change, partly by working in interdisciplinary teams and units which can bring to bear the range of relevant expertise (Pollitt, 2015a). Some PM academics are already working in these ways, but most are not. Speculatively, therefore, our megatrends may eventually lead to something of a sea change in the shape of the academic community. This is something to watch for, but also something individual scholars, reading this book, may wish to take into account for themselves. The need for solid research on the organizational implications of these four megatrends is both urgent and large.

6.10   Further reading

This chapter has been future-oriented and inherently speculative. It is not surprising, therefore, that there are no easily identifiable publications that cover all these issues in an authoritative way. My recommendations are twofold: first, follow up some of the more specific references already given at points in the preceding text; second, monitor the media for coverage of the megatrends, and note what they have to say (if anything) about the implications for public authorities.

7 Public management in interesting times

Ambitious goals contrast with the reality of a recovery that is still fragile in many places. Reforms and other essential programmes must proceed in the context of limited public investment. At the same time, societies have to urgently confront long term challenges, including sustainability and climate change. Rising inequality is also excluding large segments of society from the benefits of growth . . . The fact that trust in public institutions is strained does not make the task easier. (OECD, *Government at a Glance 2015*, p. 8)

Disatisfaction is not caused by great issues;
Nor is it primarily caused by minor concerns
It is essentially caused
By how a ruler manages things,
Wisely or otherwise,
And by what degree he commits himself – Or fails to do so.
("Announcement to Kang", in *The Most Venerable Book*, first published in 653, but in parts, including this one, probably much older. At least two attempts were made to suppress this and other historical texts on good governance – one by the First Emperor of All China, Qin Shi Huang Di in 213 BC, and the second by Chairman Mao during the Cultural Revolution of 1966–76. See Confucius, 2014, pp. ix–xi, 113)

7.1 Back to the future

This final chapter returns to the question addressed in the first chapter – what kind of a subject is PM? This question will be reassessed in the light of the intervening chapters, but also given a future twist – what kind of subject may PM be becoming? This will not, however, take the form of a prediction of one particular route. Enough has already been said to indicate that PM has never moved in just one direction in the past, and in the present is far too variegated and uncertain for the PM community suddenly to form up like a platoon and march off on a given compass bearing. Rather, I will describe certain possibilities that flow from the interaction of the internal forces currently flowing within academia and the external contexts within which PM scholars will likely find themselves.

PM is not alone in facing a difficult immediate future. Across western Europe and North America (though probably not in the BRIC countries) research monies will be harder to come by, and the management and measurement of academic life will probably continue to intensify. Yet – and here is the irony – at exactly the same time the hugely under-pressure public sector will be in ever greater need of relevant research and expertise. Meanwhile, in Brazil, India, China and elsewhere, the governments of strongly emergent economies will have to face up to the myriad problems of rapidly industrializing societies, global warming, high rates of technological change and, possibly, the construction of twenty-first-century welfare states. Their PM scholars will undoubtedly continue to learn from their colleagues in the "old west", but they will also have a long agenda of problems of their own to address.

Back to the future(s) in Europe and North America. Let us first consider the extremes. At one end of the scale there is the possibility that academic PM will simply disappear, at least as a distinct, named field. We can call this *Extinction*. Never a particularly fashionable subject, PM could suffer acutely from austerity in the university sector as well as from the widespread scepticism in some countries about governments and their capabilities. PM courses would lose their attraction and their students, PM research would fall out of favour with funding bodies. The dwindling number of new jobs in public sectors would accentuate the decline in student interest – studying PM would no longer be a sensible career option. Academic PM is not a large community – a decade or so of this kind of attrition might be enough to turn it into an ex-subject. Yet I suspect that even in this "doomsday scenario", PM would not really disappear from the university world: the label would go, but at least some of the content would remain. Scholars who analysed how organizations delivered public policies – how to budget, staff and direct them and how to hold them to account – would still be needed. These scholars might not call themselves "PM", and they might inhabit schools or departments of education or healthcare or even computer studies or environmental management – but they would still be studying the same kinds of issues which PM scholars study now. In the terms of Chapter 4, the diaspora would have become the new centre. Another part of the picture might be that staff from the present core could continue to do their work, but by operating under new management, so to speak. This has happened before – in the 1980s, for example, when some PM staff were moved out of social science departments and into business schools. Also, just outside academia, there would be a continuation of the "applied" end of PM, in the shape of the management consultancies (which show no signs of disappearing soon).

The opposite extreme might be that academic PM undergoes flowering and growth – we can call this *Expansion*. Fuelled by the megatrends of demographic change, climate change and technological innovation, realization might suddenly arrive among policymakers and students alike that here was a subject that could get to grips with the practical complexities of implementing new policies to deal with rapidly changing social, technological and environmental contexts. New courses would fill up with eager, idealistic students; research funders would rush to invest in possible organizational arrangements for dealing with the application of robots in nursing care, the promotion of sustainable public transport systems or the extreme pressures of millions of mobile and desperate migrants fleeing across national borders in order to escape war, drought and flood. In a word, PM would become fashionable – a subject that held out a reasoned prospect of fixing some of society's most visible ills.

Between extinction and high fashion lie a range of other directions. One of them, of course, is "more of the same", or *Endurance*. I must confess that it is a direction that does not overpower me with enthusiasm. My reasons for disappointment have been set out in some of the earlier chapters. First, there is the tendency for some of the leading journals in the field to retreat into a form of scholasticism in which narrow questions, methodological purity and baroque conceptualization outrank accessibility and social relevance. Second, there is the slowness to connect with some of the major external trends of our time. Governments need PM scholars as members of the team to deal with these issues, but, thus far, more of our community have wanted to immerse themselves in debates about transparency, trust and network governance than have been prepared directly to address the administrative implications of technological, demographic and climate change. Third, there is the rather limited representation of PM on those multi-disciplinary teams which are essential in addressing the "wicked problems" of our day. Whether we are looking at urban regeneration, adaptation to climate change, regulating new surveillance systems or the problems of dealing with mass immigration we tend to find (alongside the natural scientists and technologists) economists, sociologists and even political scientists, but relatively few PM scholars. This seems to be true both of purely academic project teams and advisory committees and groups set up by public authorities.

Another scenario would be for a more incremental development outwards, or *Extension*. Some PM scholars – more than in the past – would migrate to work in interdisciplinary settings, mainly concentrating on the formidable challenges posed by the external megatrends (not only the ones discussed in Chapter 6, but possibly others as well). This could build more bridges between mainline PM and parts of the PM diaspora – other professional groupings based on major public services such as healthcare, education, social care or the police and the emergency services. All these services (and more) will be grappling with demographic change, technological change, global warming and so on. PM would not in itself become fashionable, as in our *Expansion* scenario above, but it would gradually earn wider recognition as a source of indispensible advice on the processes of implementing new policies and programmes both through public agencies and through wider public-private networks and partnerships. Meanwhile the self-styled "real scientists" in PM (the positivists/deductivists) would continue along their present scholastic path, occasionally making an important contribution to the practitioner world but mainly focusing on publishing methodologically rigorous papers in a few elite journals. They would, as now, remain a minority in the PM academic community – perhaps even a dwindling minority. However, there would certainly be plenty of research puzzles for them to address, and they, too, might well orient themselves mainly outside PM (as they have often already done) towards kindred thinkers in political science, organization theory and economics. What would shrink, perhaps, would be the group within the PM community that has recently spent its time on rather abstract taxonomy-building and paradigm-debating around (inter alia) governance, networks and innovation. In hard times this might come to seem too much of a luxury, since it seldom appears to lead to either conceptual consensus or practical outcomes.

These four scenarios – *Extinction*, *Expansion*, *Endurance* and *Extension* – by no means exhaust the possibilities. There are other conceivable trajectories – indeed, this book is being written just as a new project looking at the future of PM in Europe is being launched (European Perspectives on Public Administration, www.perspectivespa.eu). But the four "Es" are at least illustrative. All, except *Extinction*, would preserve the interdisciplinary nature of PM, although the internal balance would vary considerably. Which of these directions (or which other direction) is taken will depend, in large part on the personal and career decisions of many of the readers of this book. But those individual decisions are likely to be taken within a steadily more austere structure of funding and research output measurement. The kind of delightful, blue skies' research which scholars of my generation have sometimes been privileged to indulge in will become increasingly rare. That is a great pity, because it has occasionally resulted in fascinating discoveries, quite apart from the fun of doing it. The tides, however, are running against such freedoms.

7.2   Final words

This book has been an (Advanced) Introduction. Having reached the finishing line you may have the impression that the field of PM is fairly messy, in more ways than one. To my mind that would be a realistic assessment. I hope, however, that you will also have arrived at the conclusion that the continued existence of a disciplined and independent study of how public organizations and services are managed is vitally important. It is important for academia, and for PM practitioners (whether they realize it or not!) and, ultimately, for citizens. Just as politics is, in the well-known saying, too important to be left to politicians, so are the running of our public services and the regulation of other sectors of society far too important to be left entirely to ministers, public officials and contracted-out staff. Whatever banner future PM scholars may parade beneath, they will be needed because, at their best, they can provide independent, rigorous, historically aware and comparatively nuanced analyses of many of the key elements of the policies, programmes and organizations that help to hold us together as national and local communities.

Contests between power and rationality may well be inherently weighted in favour of the former (Flyvbjerg, 1998) but that simply makes it all the more important that rationality speaks from every vantage point it can occupy. Academic PM is, in my opinion and my experience, one very significant such vantage point. It has deep intellectual fascination and profound social importance. The frustration I mentioned in my Preface comes from knowing how important this subject is, yet seeing how many powerful and intelligent people ignore or diminish it. One response to this is for the academic community to focus more sharply on how to carry out research which is relevant as well as rigorous – and to put more effort into "selling" it to politicians and public managers. This effort is underway, at least in some parts of the PM community, and we know enough already to understand that it is a long, hard road, but one not without some victories. Another response – already seen in a few instances – is to develop academic PM so that it is addressed not only to elites, but also directly to rank and file citizens. As the educational levels and digital "connectedness" of our societies rise, and as many governments become more "open" and "transparent", the future is likely offer new opportunities for PM academics to speak truth to citizens as well as to power. If PM scholars can find ways of communicating their understandings of how basic public services work, and what is required to adapt or improve them, this would surely gain the attention of many. At each election and opinion survey, millions of citizens in many countries reaffirm their high concern for healthcare, education, policing, social care and other basic public services. Interest in what is happening to local schools and hospitals, and to local crime rates, is often considerable. PM academics could become a trusted, independent source of information and analysis on these and other issues. But there is a great deal yet to be learned about communicating with different publics effectively, and hitherto this has not been a central concern for most academics. There are certainly no guarantees of success – any more than there have been when, over the years, PM academics have given advice to practitioners. Yet it is an exciting prospect: with a few local exceptions this would be the first time PM academics had been able to address citizens directly, and to seek to establish themselves as an authoritative voice in the hurly-burly of public debate.

And on this speculative note I will almost conclude. There is just one more point to be added. It brings us full circle from the Preface, where I made a similar warning myself. But this time you have it on the authority of a great philosopher:

> . . . it remains necessary to remember that no one investigator is to be trusted to give a survey of the whole field. (Bertrand Russell, cited in Raadschelders, 2011, p. 203)

References

Aberbach, J. and Rockman, B. (1987) "Comparative administration: methods, muddles and models", *Administration and Society* **18**(4), 473–506.

Alford, J. and O'Flynn, J. (2012) *Rethinking Public Service Delivery: Managing with External Providers*, Basingstoke and New York: Palgrave Macmillan.

Allison, G. and Zelikow, P. (1999) *Essence of Decision: Explaining the Cuban Missile Crisis* (2nd edn), New York: Longman.

Alvesson, M. (2002) *Postmodernism and Social Research*, Buckingham and Philadelphia, PA: Open University Press.

Andrews, M. (2013) *The Limits of Institutional Development: Changing Rules for Realistic Solutions*, Cambridge: Cambridge University Press.

Andrews, R., Boyne, G. and Walker, R. (2008) "Reconstructing empirical public administration: Lutonism or scientific realism", *Administration and Society* **40**(3), 424–30.

Argyris, C. (2000) *Flawed Advice and the Management Trap: How Managers can Know When They're Getting Good Advice and When They're Not*, Oxford: Oxford University Press.

Barrow, M. (2015) "Debate: managing motivation in hard times", *Public Money and Management* **35**(5), 329–30.

Bastow, S., Dunleavy, P. and Tinkler, J. (2014) *The Impact of the Social Sciences: How Academics and their Research Make a Difference*, London: Sage.

Bekke, H., Perry, J. and Toonen, T. (eds) (1996) *Civil Service Systems in Comparative Perspective*, Bloomington, IN: Indiana University Press.

Bekkers, V. and Homberg, V. (eds) (2005) *The Information Ecology of e-government*, Amsterdam: IOS Press.

Berg-Schlosser, D., De Meur, G., Rihoux, B. and Ragin. C. (2009) "Qualitative comparative analysis as an approach", in B. Rihoux and C. Ragin (eds) *Configurational Comparative Methods: Qualitative Comparative Analysis (QCA) and Related Techniques*, Thousand Oaks, CA and London: Sage, pp. 1–18.

Bevir, M. and Rhodes, R. (2006) *Governance Stories*, London: Routledge.

Blatter, J. and Blume, T. (2008) "In search of co-variance, causal mechanisms, or congruence? Towards a plural understanding of case studies", *Swiss Political Science Review* **14**(2), 315–56.

Blatter, J. and Haverland, M. (2012) *Designing Case Studies: Explanatory Approaches in Small-N Research*, Basingstoke: Palgrave Macmillan.

Block, P. (1999) *Flawless Consulting: A Guide to Getting Your Expertise Used* (2nd edn), New York: Jossey-Bass and Pfeiffer.

Blom-Hansen, J., Morton, R. and Serritzlew, S. (2015) "Experiments in public management research", *International Public Management Journal*, **18**(2), 151–70.

Blyth, M. (2013) *Austerity: The History of a Dangerous Idea*, Oxford: Oxford University Press.

Bogason, P. (2005) "Postmodern public administration", in E. Ferlie, L. Lynn Jr and C. Pollitt (eds) *The Oxford Handbook of Public Management*, Oxford: Oxford University Press, pp. 234–56.

Bouckaert, G. and Van de Donk, W. (eds) (2010) *The European Group for Public Administration (1975–2010) Perspectives for the Future*, Bruxelles: Bruylant.

Bovaird, T. and Löffler, E. (2003) "Evaluating the quality of public governance: indicators, models and methodologies", *International Review of Administrative Sciences* **69**(3), 313–28.

Bovens, M. (2010) "The academic advisor: professionalising commissioned research in public administration. Academically sophisticated, irrelevant to practitioners?", in G. Bouckaert and W. Van de Donk (eds) *The European Group for Public Administration (1975–2010) Perspectives for the Future*, Bruxelles: Bruylant, pp. 123–6.

Bresser-Pereira, L.C. and Spink, P. (eds) (1999) *Reforming the State: Managerial Public Administration in Latin America*, Boulder, CO: Lynne Rienner Publishers.

Brinkman, S. and Kvale, S. (2015) *Interviews: Learning the Craft of Qualitative Research Interviewing*, Thousand Oaks, CA and London: Sage.

Bulkeley, H. and Newell, P. (2010) *Governing Climate Change*, London: Routledge.

Carpenter, D. (2001) *The Forging of Bureaucratic Autonomy*, Princeton, NJ: Princeton University Press.

Cheung, A.B. (2012) "Public administration in East Asia: legacies, trajectories and lessons", *International Review of Administrative Sciences* **78**(2), 209–16.

Clarke, R.W.B. (1972) *New Trends in Government*, Civil Service College Studies No. 1, London: HMSO.

Clarke, R.W.B. (1978) *Public Expenditure, Management and Control: The Development of the Public Expenditure Survey Committee (PESC)*, London: Macmillan.

Clegg, S. and Pitsis, T. (2011) "Phronesis, projects and power research", in B. Flyvbjerg, T. Landman and S. Schram (eds) *Real Social Science: Applied Phronesis*, Cambridge: Cambridge University Press, pp. 66–91.

Commission on the Social Sciences (2003) *Great Expectations: The Social Sciences in Britain*, London: Academy of Learned Societies for the Social Sciences (http://www.the_academy.org.uk/, accessed 25 August 2015).

Confucius (ed.) (2014) *The Most Venerable Book/Shang Shu/Shu Jing* (trans. M. Palmer), London: Penguin Books.

Creel, H. (1964) "The beginnings of bureaucracy in China: the origin of the Hsien", *Journal of Asian Studies* **23**, 155–84.

Del Rosso, S.J. (2015) "Commentary: our new three Rs: rigor, relevance and readability", *Governance* **28**(2), 127–30.

Denman, R. (2002) *The Mandarin's Tale*, London: Politico's.

Di Maggio, P.J. and Powell, W.W. (1983) "The iron cage re-visited: institutional isomorphism and collective rationality in organizational fields", *American Sociological Review* **48**, 147–60.

Dixon-Woods, M., Agarwai, S., Jones, D., Young, D. and Sutton, A. (2005) "Synthesising qualitative and quantitative evidence: a review of possible methods", *Journal of Health Services Research and Policy* **10**(1), 45–53.

Douma, S. and Schreuder, H. (1998) *Economic Approaches to Organizations* (2nd edn), London and New York: Prentice Hall.

Dreschler, W. (2013) "Three paradigms of governance and administration: Chinese, Western and Islamic", Working Papers in Technology Governance and Economic Dynamics No. 50, The Other Canon Foundation, Norway.

Dunleavy, P. (1991) *Democracy, Bureaucracy and Public Choice: Economic Approaches to Political Science*, Abingdon and New York: Routledge and Taylor and Francis, reprinted in 2013, London and New York, Routledge and Taylor and Francis.

Dunleavy, P. (2003) *Authoring a Ph.D: How to Plan, Draft, Write and Finish a Doctoral Thesis or Dissertation*, Basingstoke: Palgrave Macmillan.

Dunleavy, P. and Carrera, L. (2013) *Growing the Productivity of Government Services*, Cheltenham, UK and Northampton, MA, USA: Edward Elgar.

Dunleavy. P., Margetts, H., Bastow, S. and Tinkler, J. (2006a) "New Public Management is dead – long live digital-era governance", *Journal of Public Administration Research and Theory* **16**, 467–94.

Dunleavy, P., Margetts, H., Bastow, S. and Tinkler, J. (2006b) *Digital-era Governance: IT Corporations, the State and e-government*, Oxford: Oxford University Press.

Dunsire, A. (1973) *Administration: The Word and the Science*, Oxford: Martin Robertson.

Farmer, D. (1995) *The Language of Public Administration: Bureaucracy, Modernity and Post-modernity*, Tuscaloosa, AL: University of Alabama Press.

Ferlie, E., Lynn, L. Jr and Pollitt, C. (eds) (2005) *The Oxford Handbook of Public Management*, Oxford: Oxford University Press.

Field, A. (2013) *Discovering Statistics using IBM SPSS Statistics* (4th edn), London: Sage.

Fiss, P. (2011) "Building better causal theories: a fuzzy set approach to typologies in organizational research", *Academy of Management Journal* **54**(2), 393–420.

Flinders, M. (2013) "The politics of engaged scholarship: impact, relevance and imagination", *Policy and Politics* **41**(4), 621–42.

Flyvbjerg, B. (1998) *Rationality and Power: Democracy in Practice*, Chicago, IL and London: University of Chicago Press.

Frederickson, H.G. (2005) "Whatever happened to public administration? Governance, governance everywhere", in E. Ferlie, L. Lynn Jr and C. Pollitt (eds) *The Oxford Handbook of Public Management*, Oxford: Oxford University Press, pp. 282–304.

George, A. and Bennett, A. (2005) *Case Studies and Theory Development in the Social Sciences*, Cambridge, MA: MIT Press.

Gerring, J. (2007) *Case Study Research: Principles and Practice*, Cambridge: Cambridge University Press.

Giddens, A. (2015) "The politics of climate change", *Policy and Politics* **43**(2), 155–62.

Groeneveld, S., Tummers, L., Bronkhorst, B., Ashikali, T. and Van Thiel, S. (2015) "Quantitative methods in public administration: their use and development through time", *International Public Management Journal* **18**(1), 61–86.

Guba, E.G. and Lincoln, Y. (1989) *Fourth Generation Evaluation*, New York: Sage.

Guy, M. and Rubin, M. (eds) (2015) *Public Administration Evolving: From Foundations to the Future*, New York and London: Routledge and Taylor and Francis.

Hall, P.A. (1986) *Governing the Economy: The Politics of State Intervention in Britain and France*, Oxford: Oxford University Press.

Hammond, K. (1996) *Human Judgement in Social Policy: Irreducible Uncertainty, Inevitable Error and Unavoidable Injustice*, New York and Oxford: Oxford University Press.

Harper, S. and Hamblin, K. (eds) (2014) *International Handbook on Ageing and Public Policy*, Cheltenham, UK and Northampton, MA, USA: Edward Elgar.

Hill, C.J. (2006) "Book review of 'Unleashing change: a study in organizational renewal in government', by Steven Kelman", *Journal of Policy Analysis and Management* **25**(3), 737–41.

Hirst, P. (2000) "Democracy and governance", in J. Pierre (ed.) *Debating Governance*, Oxford: Oxford University Press, pp. 13–35.

Hood, C. (1976) *The Limits of Administration*, London: Wiley.

Hood, C. (1998) *The Art of the State*, Oxford: Oxford University Press.

Hood, C. and Jackson, M. (1991) *Administrative Argument*, Aldershot: Dartmouth.

Hood, C. and Peters, G. (2004) "The middle ageing of New Public Management: into the age of paradox?", *Journal of Public Administration Research and Theory* **14**(3), 267–82.

Hood, C. and Dixon, R. (2015) *A Government that Worked Better and Cost Less? Evaluating Three Decades of Reform and Change in UK Central Government*, Oxford: Oxford University Press.

Hood, C., Heald, D. and Himaz, R. (eds) (2014) *When the Party's Over: The Politics of Fiscal Squeeze in Perspective*, Oxford: Oxford University Press for The British Academy.

Hudson, J. and Kühner, S. (2013) "Qualitative comparative analysis and applied public policy analysis: new applications of innovative methods", *Policy and Society* **32**, 279–87.

IPCC (Intergovernmental Panel on Climate Change) (2007) *Climate Change 2007: Synthesis Report*, Geneva: IPCC.

IPCC (Intergovernmental Panel on Climate Change) (2014) *Climate Change 2014: Impacts, Adaptation and Vulnerability*, Geneva: IPCC.

Jackson, B. (2001) *Management Gurus and Management Fashions*, London: Routledge.

Kahneman, D. (2012) *Thinking, Fast and Slow*, London: Penguin Books.

Kay, A. (2006) *The Dynamics of Public Policy: Theory and Evidence*, Cheltenham, UK and Northampton, MA, USA: Edward Elgar.

Keeling, D. (1972) *Management in Government*, London: Allen and Unwin.

Kelman, S. (2005) *Unleashing Change: A Study of Organizational Renewal in Government*, Washington, DC: Brookings Institution Press.

Kickert, W. and Randma-Liiv, T. (2015) *Europe Managing the Crisis: The Politics of Fiscal Consolidation*, London: Routledge and Taylor and Francis.

King, G., Keohane, R. and Verba, S. (1994) *Designing Social Enquiry: Scientific Inference in Qualitative Research*, Pinceton, NJ: Princeton University Press.

Kingdon, J. (1995) *Agendas, Alternatives and Public Policy* (2nd edn), New York: Harper Collins College Publishers.

Klein, N. (2015) *This Changes Everything* , London: Penguin Random House.

Kline, R.B. (2011) *Principles and Practice of Structural Equation Modelling*, New York: Guilford Press.

Kooiman, J. (1999) "Social-political governance: overview, reflections and design", *Public Management*, 1(1), 67–92.

Koppenjan, J. and Klijn, H.-E. (2004) *Managing Uncertainties in Networks*, London: Routledge.

KPMG (2013a) *Future State 2030: The Global Megatrends Shaping Government*, KPMG International (kpmg.com/government, accessed 4 January 2014).

KPMG (2013b) *Walking the Fiscal Tightrope: A Framework for Fiscal Sustainability in Government*, KPMG International (kpmg.com/government, accessed 4 January 2014).

Kuhlmann, S. and Wollmann, H. (2014) *Introduction to Comparative Public Administration: Administrative Systems and Reforms in Europe*, Cheltenham, UK and Northampton, MA, USA: Edward Elgar.

Kurki, M. (2008) *Causation in International Relations: Reclaiming Causal Analysis*, Cambridge: Cambridge University Press.

Landsman, T. (2008) *Issues and Methods in Comparative Politics*, London and New York: Routledge and Taylor and Francis.

Lee, J. and Reed, B. (2015) "From paper to cloud", in M. Guy and M. Rubin (eds) *Public Administration Evolving: From Foundations to the Future*, New York and London: Routledge and Taylor and Francis, pp. 158–87.

Lewis, J. (2014) "Research productivity and research system attitudes", *Public Money and Management* 34(6), 417–24.

Lijphart, A. (1999) *Patterns of Democracy: Government Forms and Performance in 36 Countries*, New Haven, CT: Yale University Press.

Luton, L. (2008) "Beyond empiricists versus postmodernists", *Administration and Society* 40(2), 211–19.

Lynn, L. Jr (2006) *Public Management: Old and New*, London and New York: Routledge and Taylor and Francis.

Lynn, L. Jr, Heinrich, C. and Hill, C. (2008) "The empiricist goose has not been cooked", *Administration and Society* 40(1), 104–9.

Ma, C., Xu, Y. and Chan, J.L. (2015) "Debate: Wang Anshi and Confucian public management – a rejoinder", *Public Money and Management* 35(4), 253–4.

Maas, A., Bodó, B., Burnley, C., Comardicia, I. and Roffey, R. (eds) (2013) *Global Environmental Change: New Drivers for Resistance, Crime and Terrorism?* Baden-Baden: Nomos.

Maggetti, M., Gilardi, F. and Radaelli, C.M. (2013) *Designing Research in the Social Sciences*, Los Angeles, CA and London: Sage.

Mahoney, J. (2000) "Strategies of causal inference in small-N analysis", *Sociological Methods and Research* 28(4), 387–424.

Mantel, H. (2009) *Wolf Hall*, New York: Henry Holt and Company.

March, J.G. (1994) *A Primer on Decision Making*, New York: The Free Press.

March, J.G. and Olsen, J.P. (1989) *Rediscovering Institutions: The Organizational Basis of Politics*, New York: The Free Press.

May, C., Finch, T. and Mort, M. (2005) "Towards a wireless patient: chronic illness, scarce care and technological innovation in the UK", *Social Science and Medicine Journal* **61**(7), 1485–94.

Mayer-Schönberger, V. and Cukier, K. (2013) *Big Data: A Revolution that Will Transform How We Live, Work and Think*, New York: Houghton Mifflin Harcourt.

Meyer, R.E. and Rowan, B. (1977) "Institutional organizations: formal structure as myth and ceremony", *American Journal of Sociology* **83**, 340–63.

Ministry of Finance (2013) *Governments for the Future: Main Report*, Helsinki: Ministry of Finance (http://www.vm.fi/vm/fi/04_julkaisut_ja_asiakirjat/01_julkaisut/08_muut_julkaisut/20131119Govern/Government_for_the_Future.pdf, accessed 4 January 2014).

Morgan, D.L. (2014) *Integrating Qualitative and Quantitative Methods: A Pragmatic Approach*, Thousand Oaks, CA: Sage.

Mungiu-Pippidi, A. (2015) *The Quest for Good Governance: How Societies Develop Control of Corruption*, Cambridge: Cambridge University Press.

National Audit Office (2006) *Central Government's Use of Consultants*, HC128, Session 2006-7, London: The Stationery Office.

Nemec, J., Spacek, D., Suway, P. and Modrejewski, A. (2012) "Public management as a university discipline in new European Union member states: the central European case", *Public Management Review* **14**(8), 1087–8.

OECD (2015) *Government at a Glance 2015*, Paris: OECD.

O'Toole, L.J. Jr and Meier, K.J. (2003) "*Plus ça change*: public management, personnel stability and organizational performance", *Journal of Public Administration Research and Theory* **13**(1), 43–64.

Osborne, S. (ed.) (2010) *The New Public Governance? Emerging Perspectives on the Theory and Practice of Public Governance*, Abingdon: Routledge and Taylor and Francis.

Pawson, R. (2013) *The Science of Evaluation: A Realist Manifesto*, Los Angeles, CA and London: Sage.

Perry, J.L. and Hondeghem, A. (eds) (2008) *Motivation in Public Management: The Call of Public Service*, Oxford: Oxford University Press.

Perry, J., Engbers, T. and Jun, S. (2009) "Back to the future? Performance-related pay, empirical research, and the perils of persistance", *Public Administration Review* **69**(1), 39–51.

Perry, J.L., Hondeghem, A. and Wise, L. (2010) "Revisiting the motivational basis of public service: twenty years of research and an agenda for the future", *Public Administration Review* **70**(5), 681–90.

Peters, G.B. (1996) "Theory and methodology", in H. Bekke, J. Perry and T. Toonen (eds) *Civil Service Systems in Comparative Perspective*, Bloomington, IN: Indiana University Press, pp. 13–41.

Peters, G.B. (1997) "A North American perspective on administrative modernisation in Europe", in W. Kickert (ed.) *Public Management and Administrative Reform in Western Europe*, Cheltenham, UK and Northampton, MA, USA: Edward Elgar, pp. 255–70.

Peters, G.B. (2000) *Institutional Theory in Political Science: The New Institutionalism*, London: Continuum.

Petrovsky, N. and Avellaneda, C. (2014) "Mayoral public sector work experience and tax collection performance in Colombian local governments", *International Public Management Journal* **17**(2), 145–73.

Pierre, J. and Ingraham, P. (eds) (2010) *Comparative Administrative Change and Reform: Lessons Learned*, Montreal: McGill-Queen's University Press.

Pierson, P. (2004) *Politics in Time: History, Institutions and Social Anlaysis*, Princeton, NJ: Princeton University Press.

Pollitt, C. (2003) *The Essential Public Manager*, Buckingham and Philadelphia, PA: Open University Press.

Pollitt, C. (2008) *Time, Policy, Management: Governing with the Past*, Oxford: Oxford University Press.

Pollitt, C. (2010) "Simply the best? The international benchmarking of reform and good governance", in J. Pierre and P. Ingraham (eds) *Comparative Administrative Change and Reform: Lessons Learned*, Montreal and Kingston: McGill-Queen's University Press, pp. 91–113.

Pollitt, C. (2011) "Not odious but onerous: comparative public administration", *Public Administration* **89**(1), 114–27.

Pollitt, C. (2012) *New Perspectives on Public Services: Place and Technology*, Oxford: Oxford University Press.

Pollitt, C. (ed.) (2013a) *Context in Public Policy and Management: The Missing Link?* Cheltenham, UK and Northampton, MA, USA: Edward Elgar.

Pollitt, C. (2013b) "The evolving narratives of public management reform", *Public Management Review* **15**(6), 899–922.

Pollitt, C. (2014) *Future Trends in European Public Administration and Management: An Outside-in Perspective*, COCOPS Report – Work Package 8, April (http://www.cocops.eu, accessed 7 February 2015).

Pollitt, C. (2015a) "Wickedness will not wait: climate change and public management research", *Public Money and Management* **35**(3), 181–6.

Pollitt, C. (2015b) "Towards a new world: some inconvenient truths for Anglosphere public administration", *International Review of Administrative Sciences* **81**(1), 3–17.

Pollitt, C. and Bouckaert, G. (2009) *Continuity and Change in Public Policy and Management*, Cheltenham, UK and Northampton, MA, USA: Edward Elgar.

Pollitt, C. and Bouckaert, G. (2011) *Public Management Reform: A Comparative Analysis: New Public Management, Governance and the Neo-Weberian State* (3rd edn), Oxford: Oxford University Press.

Pollitt, C. and Hupe, P. (2011) "Talking about government: the role of magic concepts", *Public Management Review* **89**(1), 114–27.

Pollitt, C. and Op de Beeck, L. (2010) *Training Top Civil Servants: A Comparative Analysis*, Leuven: Instituut voor de Overheid, Katholieke Universiteit Leuven.

Raadschelders, J.C. (2010) "Is American public administration detached from historical context? On the nature of time and the need to understand it in government and its study", *American Review of Public Administration* **40**(3), 235–60.

Raadschelders, J.C. (2011) *Public Administration: The Interdisciplinary Study of Government*, Oxford: Oxford University Press.

Raadschelders, J.C. and Lee, K.-H. (2011) "Trends in the study of public administration: empirical and qualitative observations from *Public Administration Review*, 2000–2009", *Public Administration Review* **71**(1), 19–33.

Radin, B. (2013) "Reclaiming our past: linking theory and practice" (the 2012 John Gaus Lecture), *Political Science and Politics* **46**(01), January, 1–7.

Rainey, H. (1997) *Understanding and Managing Public Organizations* (2nd edn), San Francisco, CA: Jossey-Bass.

Rainey, H. and Bozeman, B. (2000) "Comparing public and private organizations: empirical research and the power of the a priori", *Journal of Public Administration Research and Theory* **10**(2), 447–69.

Randma-Liiv, T., Nakrosis, V. and Hajnal, G. (2011) "Public sector organization in Central and Eastern Europe: from agencification to de-agencification", *Transylvanian Review of Administrative Sciences*, Special Issue, 60–175.

Ranson, S. and Stewart, J. (1994) *Managing in the Public Domain: Enabling the Learning Society*, Basingstoke: Macmillan.

Reissman, C. (2008) *Narrative Methods for the Human Sciences*, Thousand Oaks, CA: Sage.

Rhodes, R. (1997) *Understanding Governance*, Buckingham: Open University Press.

Rhodes, R.A.W. (2000) "Governance and public administration", in J. Pierre (ed.) *Debating Governance*, Oxford: Oxford University Press, pp. 54–90.

Rhodes, R. (2007) "Understanding governance: ten years on", *Organization Studies* **28**(8), 1–22.

Rhodes, R. (2010) "Public administration", in G. Bouckaert and W. Van de Donk (eds) *The European Group for Public Administration (1975–2010) Perspectives for the Future*, Bruxelles: Bruylant, pp. 26–30.

Rhodes, R. (2011) "Thinking on: a career in public administration", *Public Administration* **89**(1), 196–212.

Rhodes, R., Dargie, C., Melville, A. and Tutt, B. (1995) "The state of public administration: a professional history, 1970–1995", *Public Administration* **73**(1), 1–15.

Riccucci, N.M. (2010) *Public Administration: Traditions of Inquiry and Philosophies of Knowledge*, Washington, DC: Georgetown University Press.

Rihoux, B. and Ragin, C. (eds) (2009) *Configurational Comparative Methods: Qualitative Comparative Analysis (QCA) and Related Techniques*, Thousand Oaks, CA and London: Sage.

Robson, C. (2002) *Real World Research: A Resource for Social Scientists and Practitioner-Researchers* (2nd edn), Malden, MA: Blackwell Publishing.

Rohr, J. (2002) *Civil Servants and their Constitutions*, Lawrence, KS: University Press of Kansas.

Royal Netherlands Academy of Arts and Sciences (2005) *Wetenschap op beselling-over de omgang tussen wetenschappelijk onderzoekers en hun opdrachtgevers* (*Research Made to Order – the Relationship Between Researchers and their Clients*), Amsterdam: KNAW.

Ruel, E., Wagner III, W.E. and Gillespie, J. (2015) *The Practice of Survey Research: Theory and Applications*, Thousand Oaks, CA: Sage.

Rueschemeyer, D. (2003) "Can one or a few cases yield theoretical gains?", in J. Mahoney and D. Rueschemeyer (eds) *Comparative Historical Analysis in the Social Sciences*, Cambridge: Cambridge University Press, pp. 305–36.

Rutgers, M. (2001) "Traditional flavours? The different sentiments in European and American administrative thought", *Administration and Society* **33**(2), 220–44.

Sahlin-Andersson, K. and Engwall, L. (2002) *The Expansion of Management Knowledge: Carriers, Flows and Sources*, Stanford, CA: Stanford University Press.

Saint-Martin, D. (2000) *Building the New Managerialist State: Consultants and the Politics of Public Sector Reform in Comparative Perspective*, Oxford: Oxford University Press.

Schram, S. (2012) "Phronetic social science: an idea whose time has come", in B. Flyvbjerg, T. Landman and S. Schram (eds) *Real Social Science: Applied Phronesis*, Cambridge: Cambridge University Press, pp. 15–26.

Simon, H. (1946) "Proverbs of administration", *Public Administration Review* **6** (Winter), 53–67.

Smullen, A. (2010) *Translating Agency Reform: Rhetoric and Culture in Comparative Perspective*, Basingstoke: Palgrave Macmillan.

Snellen, I. and Van de Donk, W. (eds) (1998) *Public Administration in an Information Age: A Handbook*, Amsterdam: IOS Press.

Stillman, R. (2015) "Foreword", in M. Guy and M. Rubin (eds) *Public Administration Evolving: From Foundations to the Future*, New York and London: Routledge and Taylor and Francis, pp. x–xix.

Streeck, W. and Thelen, K. (eds) (2005) *Beyond Continuity: Institutional Change in Advanced Political Economies*, Oxford: Oxford University Press.

Sundström, G. (2006) "Management by results: its origin and development in the case of the Swedish state", *International Public Management Journal* **9**(4), 399–427.

Taliercio, R. Jr (2004) "The design, performance and sustainability of semi-autonomous revenue authorities in Africa and Latin America", in C. Pollitt and C. Talbot (eds) *Unbundled Government: A Critical Analysis of the Global Trend to Agencies, Quangos and Contractualisation*, London and New York: Routledge and Taylor and Francis, pp. 264–82.

Termeer, C., Dewulf, A., Van Rijswick, H. et al. (2011) "The regional governance of climate change: a framework for developing legitimate, effective, and resilient governance arrangements", *Climate Law* **2**, 159–79.

Thatcher, M. (2002) "Delegation to independent regulatory agenices: pressures, functions and contextual mediation", *West European Politics* **25**(1), 125–47.

Tummers, L. and Bekkers, V. (2014) "Policy implementation, street-level bureaucracy, and the importance of discretion", *Public Management Review* **16**(4), 527–47.

Van de Walle, S. and Van Delft, R. (2015) "Publishing in public administration: issues with defining, comparing, and ranking the outputs of universities", *International Public Management Journal* **18**(1), 87–107.

Van Thiel, S. (2014) *Research Methods in Public Administration and Public Management: An introduction*, London and New York: Routledge and Taylor and Francis.

Van Wart, M., Hondeghem, A. and Schwella, E. (eds) (2015) *Leadership and Culture: Comparative Models of Top Civil Service Training*, Basingstoke and New York: Palgrave Macmillan.

Whetsell, T. and Shields, P. (2015) "The dynamics of positivism in the study of public administration: a brief intellectual history and reappraisal", *Administration and Society* **47**(4), 416–46.

Wildavsky, A. (1979) *Speaking Truth to Power; The Art and Craft of Policy Analysis*, Boston, MA: Little, Brown and Co.

Wilks, S. (2013) *The Political Power of the Business Corporation*, Cheltenham, UK and Northampton, MA, USA: Edward Elgar.

Wilson, J.Q. (1989) *Bureaucracy*, New York: Basic Books.

Wright Mills, C. (1959) *The Sociological Imagination*, New York: Oxford University Press, reprinted in 2000.

Yang, K. (2015) "From administration to management", in M. Guy and M. Rubin (eds) *Public Administration Evolving: From Foundations to the Future*, New York and London: Routledge and Taylor and Francis, pp. 102–22.

Yin, R.K. (2014) *Case Study Research: Design and Methods* (5th edn), Thousand Oaks, CA: Sage.

Zalmanovitch, Y. (2014) "Don't reinvent the wheel: the search for an identity for public administration", *International Review of Administrative Sciences* **80**(4), 808–26.

Index